Love. Loss. Life.

First published by MFBooks Joburg,
an imprint of Jacana Media (Pty) Ltd, in 2014

10 Orange Street
Sunnyside
Auckland Park 2092
South Africa
+2711 628 3200
www.jacana.co.za

ISBN 978-1-920601-48-5

Cover design by publicide
Set in Sabon 11/15pt
Printed and bound by Creda Communications
Job no. 002266

See a complete list of Jacana titles at www.jacana.co.za

Love. Loss. Life.

Monica Nicolson Oosterbroek
Hilton-Barber Zwolsman

MF BOOKS JOBURG

All the world's a stage
And all the men and women merely players
They have their exits and their entrances
And one man in his time plays many parts.

– Act 2, Scene 7, *As You Like It*,
WILLIAM SHAKESPEARE

For my mum –
Elizabeth Stewart Davidson Nicolson –
for her unconditional love and support always

Acknowledgements

Thanks always to my mum, for inspiring and encouraging me to be a better person.

I am also deeply grateful to my dad, Ronald Nicolson, who read my entire book with only love in his heart, and gave me invaluable advice without judgement.

Special love for Gail, my other mother, who has picked me up so many times in the last 30 years, who packed up my home and contents three times, who has flown across the world several times on different occasions to support me in difficult times, and with whom I have so many treasured memories.

I am also deeply grateful for my much-loved siblings: Andrew, for standing right next to me and holding me up more than a few times; Catherine for looking after me in Australia; Simon for uncritically understanding me and staying with me after Steven died; and Lucy for living with me after Ken died and sharing so much laughter and fun in our overlapping Johannesburg and Durban days. Thanks also to Welma who generously opened her heart and home to me and my tribe after Steven and Benjamin died.

I also want to thank Robin Comley, an unsung hero of the Johannesburg newspaper world, who made my life so much easier by protecting me from my harsh critics and life's unkind people, and for always having my best interests at heart.

For my extra-special support crew: Debbie Christy, Bridget, Dave, Brett and Josie Hilton-Barber, Justine Speed, Alison Dow, Kate Chipman, Fiona Irvine, Shelagh Foster, Kate Hawkins, Maureen Isaacson, Geri, Ath, Estelle, Les and Con Oosterbroek and relatives, the special Pox Bush, Rick Morton, and Seema Reynolds, who shared with me the value of telling our stories through writing.

All the many magnificent women – who wrote letters, phoned, invited me to dinner, kept up with me on Facebook, sent messages of love, posted inspirational poems, CDs, shared their memories and their stories – thanks to the Sisterhood far and wide who have reached out to me when the going got tough and who played such a vital role in the story of my survival.

Many thanks to Pam Hamilton, super-cool guardian of Ken's and Steven's pictures and my loyal friend.

The Gold Coast Bahá'í community. May our actions each and every day be beautiful prayers.

To my Mothers' Club – Kimbra, Jonene, Megan, Mike, April and Tony.

Vicky Kersey who carefully read the first draft and gave me objective advice.

And to Melinda Ferguson, whose own powerful story inspired me to tell my own. Thanks for all your love, encouragement and support through this process.

Lastly, and most importantly, to Yannik and Soren, who I love from here past the Clouds of Magellan to the end of the universe and beyond.

Preface

Hanging out my private life and intimate feelings for public consumption is slightly awkward and embarrassing. My life has been an incredible journey – where fate and personal choice have met with tragic results – and a survival story I never imagined writing.

Despite teetering often on the brink of eternal darkness, I've discovered that the body's natural life force is impossible to quench, and that life is about deep love, beautiful new beginnings and constant renewal of hope.

This book tries to find answers and meaning to surviving the temporary nature of my existence on earth, but I also want to reach out to others who have experienced turmoil and trauma in their lives. I've looked over the edge to see nothing but hopelessness and despair on many occasions, but I continue to bounce back. Picked up by love and support, I am happily marching forward into the future.

My survival is a tribute to my family, friends, and lots of women. The love and support, help and companionship received in all stages of my life from *les femmes* old, new and strange, leaves me grateful and humble. I salute you all.

Stories and people are like prisms. It depends on where the light strikes as to what colour shines out. This is just my ray of truth; my story, and part of history seen through my eyes. My facts don't change, but my opinions and perspective are constantly shifting, changing and evolving. So this is only how I feel about my life at this stage in my life.

Life is like a river: ever moving forward, changing, twisting and turning until it flows into the sea and back into itself again.

Prologue

I ran to the beach and flung myself onto the sand.

"Fuck you, God, how can you do this to me?" I screamed up at the sky. "I want to die."

I did. I really, really wanted to kill myself. I lay there sobbing and screaming until I ran out of breath.

I planned to die. This time I no longer cared about how it might hurt my parents or my brothers and sisters. I imagined driving off in my camper van and gassing myself by taking handfuls of sleeping tablets and turning on the indoor gas stove. I felt no remorse, no fright, only a bone-deep weary sadness.

But, as I grappled with the logistics, I realised I couldn't possibly leave my sons behind to pick up the emotional pieces, I couldn't scar them for life with this monumental burden. They would have to come with me. I'd save them from having to live in this horrible world where they too would only be hurt and crushed.

"Haha, God," I thought. "I'll take them first before you can … This time I will be in control of death."

In every previous knockdown punch life had landed on me, I had always known deep down that I would get right back up. The light of possibility and beauty of existence always shone, even though sometimes it was so very, very dim.

But now I felt out for the count. Madness had come to visit. It felt like my life was over.

Chapter 1

I was attracted to Ken the minute I saw him. I first caught a glimpse of this long-haired photographer while covering a court case in Randburg. Tall, dark and brooding, with a restless energy and intensity, here was my vision of Emily Brontë's Heathcliff. Young enough to be impressed by his carefully cultivated and stereotypical photographer look – black peak cap on back-to-front, scruffy jeans and boots, camera jacket and cameras slung over his shoulders – here was my idea of gorgeous.

"Who's that?" I asked the photographer I was on the news assignment with.

"Oh, that's Ken Oosterbroek," was the reply. "He's really full-on."

A week later, we met again.

On my first day at *The Star* I swanned in, covering my nervousness with my annoying in-your-face bravado and check-me-out attitude. And there my mysterious man was, waiting for me. We'd been assigned together to cover a break-and-enter where the homeowner had been shot. As we arrived at the home, police had cordoned off the area and ambulance men were loading someone into an ambulance. Ken leapt from the car, over the yellow barrier tape, and started taking photographs, which immediately infuriated police who sent us packing.

My modus operandi would have been to approach the cops politely, get the relevant information, and then Ken could have aggressively pursued the pictures. His way meant I got no law enforcement cooperation and had to rely on news gleaned from witnesses, and descriptions from bystanders.

"What the hell are you doing, you idiot?" I fumed afterwards. "What is your problem?"

We drove back to *The Star* in brittle silence.

As I was filing my copy, which included writing photo captions and by-lines, Ken hovered at my desk, peering over my shoulder to make sure I was spelling his name correctly.

"Big O, little O," he started to say.

Ken had recently won his first Press Photographer of the Year award and was clearly a bit up himself, extra eager that I understand how important he was. I, on the other hand, had just come from the smaller and less prestigious *Citizen* newspaper but had inflated opinions of my own fabulousness.

"You are fucking irritating me," I snapped. "Just piss off and leave me alone."

"Don't treat me like I'm just a photographer – I've been around longer than you, so you just look and learn," he hissed back.

We then launched into an argument so heated that the assistant editor walked out of his office to ask what the hell was going on.

From the get-go, the chemistry was there and that day marked the start of a most passionate and volatile relationship.

Later that afternoon when I packed up, Ken stopped by my desk and said he'd walk me down to the car park at the Market Theatre, down in Newtown in the Johannesburg CBD, where I was parked.

"It's dangerous past the bus rank this time of day," he said. "Another journo was attacked there last week."

And so he made sure he was around to walk me down every day for the next fortnight – and then every day possible for the rest of the time I worked there.

We went on our first 'date' when he invited me to a music session at the Market Theatre. I turned up with washed and brushed hair flying everywhere, shaved legs and armpits, and jeans with a T-shirt so as to look casually relaxed. I forget who was playing but it was some jazzy thang, which I had pretended to like to seem cool. We chatted about our job and some of the stories we had worked on, me waving my hands about animatedly and flirting madly, and we talked about our families. Watching him buying a bottle of wine and walking back to our table, I saw him trip and fall, miraculously saving the wine from spilling. I kindly pretended not to notice as even then I knew he was not a person to easily laugh at himself.

When I started at *The Star* at the very beginning of 1990, Ken told the entire photographic department, "Hands off, she's mine." On Valentine's Day, which also happened to be Ken's birthday, he left a card on my desk saying: "You are not my Valentine" and as I turned the page it said "… yet." I was deeply thrilled and flattered even though I was still happily engaged to my university sweetheart, Pete.

In March 1990, Ken invited me to accompany him to a wedding he was photographing for friends up in the Northern Transvaal.

"Honey, I have to go away this weekend, on an assignment … travel story in the Northern Transvaal," I lied to my fiancé.

Despite being riddled with guilt, Ken and I laughed the entire trip there over nothing and everything, and as soon as it became too dark to photograph the wedding any more and I'd had a few glasses of wine, we started kissing – and by the end of the weekend, I was fully infatuated. The love endorphins were so high, I didn't blink an eye at lions roaring in the camp site, or a bee stinging me in the mouth when I took a bite of wedding cake the next morning.

The following weekend, Kevin Carter, myself and Ken piled into my tiny Mazda 323 (a car my fiancé had bought) and headed off to Namibia to cover the Namibian Independence celebrations. Kevin was Ken's best friend, the first person Ken introduced me to when we started dating. Kevin and his girlfriends (ever-changing) often hung out with Ken and me in the early days. The 'brothers' had met a few years previously when they were both at similar stages in their lives. They looked alike, with dark-brown hair in mullet style, same height and weight, both dressed in tight stovepipe jeans, long-sleeved T-shirts with a short T-shirt over, caps and cameras. Their shared passion for photography fuelled mutual ambitions and big dreams with all the passion of 20-something young men. For the first couple of years they were inseparable, either working or getting stoned and talking about photographs.

That weekend, Ken and I danced and filed copy and had sex. There I was, actually now being physically unfaithful to my fiancé, and my emotions were all over the place. To make things even more awkward, Kevin was hugely pissed off that I'd chosen Ken over him, and for the entire awkward journey back from Swakopmund to Johannesburg, Kevin sat in the back seat, sulking in stony silence like a petulant child. Ken and Kevin didn't talk for a few weeks.

Moving out from Pete's was awful. To this day I feel guilty for causing Pete pain. I did love him, but there wasn't the passion and drama I needed at that stage of my life … he was just a darling boy who cherished me. And I adored him right back, but I had this desperate need for adventure and craziness. He was offering love and stability and normality in suburbia – kids, dogs, Sandton City and holidays at the beach. I wanted adrenalin-fuelled madness.

I returned home to find him sitting and waiting for me, tear-stained, white with worry, and truly heartbroken. This is a guy who'd stood by me and my brothers and sisters when our parents divorced, through all my unsettled university days, supporting me financially and emotionally. That day, however, Pete realised our engagement was over. Yet he continued to be so generous and kind, helping me move out into a share-house in Houghton, where I stayed for three months with a rather motley crew of weird people.

For six months, I was torn between wanting to settle down and be 'normal' with my fiancé to whom I was deeply attached, and falling intensely in love with Ken.

"I am head over heels in love with a glorious man who has arrested my heart, blown my mind and set my body alight with

extreme emotion," I wrote in my diary. Yes, I know, it's not exactly Shakespeare, but I was just a young girl in love with no real writing skills yet to express myself more eloquently.

Ken, on the other hand, didn't feel that secure and was really fazed by my continued bond with Pete. He'd leave me poems he wrote, like:

"Rome was not built in a day

"Or maybe in any way.

"Is there real brick in this Colosseum of love, or is it a castle made of air?

"Monica Jane Moho

"Be real, I wish to feel capital letters, not question marks."

I'd vacillate between Ken and Pete – wanting both worlds – and hurting both in the process. On occasion, especially when Ken was late for a date or didn't run around my every need with enough speed and enthusiasm, I would 'break up' with him. And he would leave sad notes like:

"I thought I was fucked up when I met you. It's got nothing on now. Now I have what I didn't before, but not things which I had. What I can't do is let you run into the night. If we are to part, it will be in the cold reality of day. It doesn't matter what you think of me anyway – you can't communicate it to me. I will always love you. Remember that."

Our first year was crazy. When I met him he was a dope smoker and for me that was utterly terrifying. He confessed to me once he'd taken LSD as a teenager at a music festival, and I was so completely shocked and horrified I cried for days. I am the daughter of a former Anglican minister and grew up in a home where I remember neither parent drinking alcohol. I certainly didn't drink much. Yes, I had smoked a joint or two and perhaps drunk too much wine a few times in my university days – but I had loathed both. So this was all very frightening for me.

And the fact he had a daughter from a previous relationship also did my head in. Before we even got involved, I told him his being a father was a non-negotiable and that he'd have to choose between her and me – that I wasn't sharing him with anyone – one of several things we'd later argue passionately about.

Four months after meeting Ken, we started living together. This was partly because I was staying in a strange commune in Houghton and he was sharing a flat with his older brother, who drank ferociously and insisted on smoking mandrax even when I visited Ken. Ken was fed up with being woken up at all hours to his brother's crazed rantings and ravings. One night Ken's brother sat up a tree, shouting and screaming abuse at us until the early hours of the morning. So Ken and I moved into a flat together.

One of our first holidays as a couple involved heading off to the Karoo to pick up his kombi, which had blown up there before we met and the engine was being overhauled. We caught the train down and spent a glorious week getting there and back, laughing and loving and being silly.

In October 1990, we took off in the kombi for a three-week road trip to the West Coast, with only a mattress in the back and rudimentary camping equipment, plus loads of cameras and film.

"Johannesburg seems a million miles away, our lives there a vague, distant and depressing reality.

"Here, time is irrelevant, drifting from consciousness to sleep and satisfying only our basic urges – eat, drink, make love and sleep.

"Just vast open spaces, endless kms of deserted barren wasteland, rocks, sand dunes, cold sea and wind.

"Sun and wind melt and blow away tension ... muscles heavy, mind lethargic.

"Today, I wish I didn't even have to think about the future, just live for the day – and leave destiny to take over – just want an insulated isolated existence with just me, my Ken O and our actual environment out here on the West Coast.

"Watching the sun rise, catching the white of the waves, mysterious magical shimmering surface under pink clouds ... endless opening of gates on side roads, rescuing tortoises from the road, eating fish, pulling mussels off rocks.

"I love my Keno – so patient, tender, loving ... so demanding and proud – turning brown and healthy in the sun ... his long,

lean body moving perfectly, head bending over tasks, his face set in concentration, totally absorbed … watching his fringe standing up stiff with sea salt and errant bits flopping round his face.

"Out here in the West Coast with no pressure, we click together and hum along in harmony … I adore this strange man."

We became a world absorbed in each other, with not a lot left over outside work and us. We filled our life with joyful exuberance – I loved that he'd throw his head back and belly laugh with his eyes crinkling up with mirth and body rocking to and fro – and we did everything together, including household chores and laundry. He'd get drunk and I'd sling him over my shoulder at The Liz, the bar across the road from *The Star* newspaper in Sauer Street, and carry him out. We often took off camping for a night where we'd simply drive and stop wherever took our fancy. On one such trip, we got bust having sex in public. Well, to explain, it was very dark when we stopped – and then it quickly became light – and a policeman was patrolling an isolated car park in Ogies near Middelburg and spied us in the van. But we giggled about it for a long, long time afterwards – even after we got fined for public indecency.

In retrospect, I must have been a bit of an embarrassment to Ken. His public persona was fully serious and he was crafting an image of valuable newsman and all-over cool guy. I, conversely, was quite silly. I read Mills & Boon romance novels, even in public, and my taste in music then gravitated more to John Denver, Celine Dion and Whitney Houston. He read *Newsweek* and I read *You* magazine. It wasn't easy for him to dance cheek to cheek with me at a Chris de Burgh concert in front of his colleagues, but he did it, cringingly, because he loved me.

On the other hand, I spent hours and hours standing around waiting for him to take pictures. Everywhere we went, I waited, nearly always patiently. In fact, on a trip to Holland where Ken was collecting a World Press Photo award, I spent so much time in Amsterdam's Red Light District standing around while Ken took pictures, I think people believed I was flaunting my wares.

Our early days were tempestuous and volatile. I'd deliberately make him jealous – my childish insecurities forced him to prove over and over again I was Number One in his life. So I danced nose to nose with Kevin (Carter), which led to them having a punch-up fight. I visited my ex, Pete, and Ken smashed his camera against a wall. I'd throw glasses of wine in any woman's face if she spent more than a few seconds talking to Ken at a party. I threatened to end the relationship because he was late for a movie date, so Ken collected all the money he'd earned working overtime to buy me a leather jacket, then he put it in a bowl, and set fire to it. Nearly R1 000 went up in smoke.

I banned him from his past life of drugs and drug-taking family members. I felt some of his records had an evil drug-based culture and frisbeed them out of the window of our flat. And, to my shame, I forced his baby daughter to have a blood test to prove to me and him she was in fact his daughter. The image I still have is of me angrily watching this baby screaming and being held down by her traumatised mother, Ken looking stricken, and I absolutely didn't care about their pain. Wow, that completely shocks me now that I was me.

But my dramatics were never-ending. Ken left me standing alone in a bar one night while he went outside to talk to some skanky-looking friend – and I stomped off in a huff.

"Get in the damn car," Ken said as I marched along the main road. He'd soon noticed I'd gone and had rushed after me in his kombi.

I refused.

Next thing, the police pulled up.

"Madam, are you okay?" they asked.

"No," I cried. "This strange man is trying to make me get in his car."

With that, Ken drove off and the police offered to take me home.

Unfortunately, that stunt backfired on me. Ken had the flat keys and as I stood at the door with the police watching me and wondering what to do, Ken arrived and opened up.

We'd fight – then make up. The reconciling was always overwhelmingly sweet.

Surprisingly, our relationship was never under threat of combusting. I was madly, crazily in love with him – an inexplicable passion of momentous proportions. So when he asked me to marry him, I said yes. Of course.

Chapter 2

I was born the year after South African icon Nelson Mandela was imprisoned. My childhood was tainted with the horrors of apartheid at its worst, with pass laws, forced removals, the State of Emergency, the student uprising in Soweto and the homeland policy.

I was the second born after my brother, Andrew. After me is Catherine, 15 months my junior, followed by 'the babies' a few years later, Simon and Lucy. We were like a basket of warm puppies, all cuddly and boisterous, fiercely guarded by our mother, Elizabeth, who cared for us full-time. Dad, a Doctor of Divinity, spent the first years of my life as an Anglican minister in the small town of Howick in the Natal Midlands.

Like so many white children living in Natal, we were raised on *Winnie the Pooh*, *Paddington Bear*, *Wind in the Willows* and *The Secret Garden*. I was continually homesick for my idea of England, a world of fairies in meadows, Wombles on commons, roses and robins and white Christmases with the Cambridge Boys' Choir and Westminster Abbey.

Yet we also grew up with National Party apartheid guardians Adriaan Vlok, BJ Vorster, PW Botha and the threat of the Cold War from abroad. I learnt to fear police and the government. As kids, my siblings and I proudly told people how our dad was beaten up by security police when he jumped onto a stage where Hendrik

Verwoerd was about to speak to protest against his policies at a National Party rally in the '50s. Or that government spies probably listened in to his sermons on Sundays. I adored that he might be important enough for the government to be keeping tabs on.

Yet we feared the Red under our bed. At night, when our parents were out, my elder brother and sister would sit on my bed looking out at the black night, wondering if "terrorists or communists" were going to break in and kill us, freezing at every rustle or crackle outside.

My first memories of black people were Joshua and Norah, the gardener and domestic worker who lived in the khaya (outside room) at the bottom of our lush, green garden, and both of whom came as part and parcel of the rectory.

As toddlers, we'd eagerly follow Joshua round the garden all day, intrigued by leather discs the size of Marie biscuits in his ear lobes and his earthy smell of wet leaves, tobacco and smoky wood fires. A traditional Zulu, he spoke little English and politely tolerated us, then disappeared each Christmas to his family on a farm somewhere mysterious. One day, he took off for his Christmas break and only returned many months later. The reason he disappeared remained a mystery to us children, and even though we asked, the answer was not considered our childish business.

Norah, a young Zulu woman, was more fun and teasingly threatened to breast-feed us, chasing us round the house squirting us with her breast milk. Where her own baby lived was a mystery to us. We never saw the baby and she never wanted to talk about it, brushing off our questions with vague ambiguity.

We'd go down the back of the garden, past the compost heap and coal shed, round the mossy-bricked garage, to peep into the world where Norah and Joshua lived at night. But it was a dark and forbidden territory where we quickly lost courage and fled back to the safety of our red-polished back veranda.

My first memories are of my horrible fear of losing a member of my family. From as young as five years old, I'd repeatedly dream of me, my parents, two brothers and two sisters being forced to cross a rickety bridge over a deep canyon. (Thank you, *Bridge on the*

River Kwai!) I can still recall my terror of watching each member wobble precariously across – and fighting to wake up, sweating and panic-stricken, newly aware that I couldn't control my world.

I dreaded the day we'd all grow up and fly the nest. I wanted to keep us all together forever. I'd dream of buying a huge commune where we could all live with our spouses, kids and dogs. I wished to wrap us all up in cosy seclusion away from the menacing big world beyond.

My life took its first downward spiral when I was six, when we left the garden of bountiful fruit trees, massive oaks and hydrangea bushes in Howick for the grey industrial town of Pinetown outside Durban. Our family moved to a new rectory alongside the main highway. A man had been bludgeoned to death by an armed burglar in our derelict new home and the walls had to be whitewashed to cover the blood, something adults spoke of in whispers. Massive rats nested in our cupboards and ran over our faces at night, and the cracked linoleum on the kitchen floor was black with age-old grime. Crying, we left Norah and Joshua behind, and we never had domestic help again. My mother did everything around the house, including the garden. She didn't want the shuffling of strange bare feet invading her privacy; she felt uncomfortable giving orders to anyone bar us kids, and we simply couldn't afford to house or feed any extra people on the tiny church stipend.

So our world was eerily white, except for watching the occasional busload of 'blacks' racing past on the highway in dilapidated green buses billowing smoke, and us standing at the bottom of our garden waving to Indian school kids in their buses with colourful adornments, glittery decorations and Eastern music blaring.

I didn't know any Afrikaners when I was young, yet believed they were inferior to all South Africans. To us kids, they were the source of much amusement, to be mocked at every opportunity. We delighted in all the Van der Merwe jokes where the Afrikaner male was depicted as a racist buffoon with no intelligence. And any school outing was great sport if it crossed paths with Afrikaans kids from the Afrikaans schools of Port Natal or Dirkie Uys (Dirty

Face) government school, with their supposedly thick ankles, massive necks and cauliflower ears.

Afrikanerdom to us was a world of *koeksusters*, doilies, plastic table clothes, lace curtains and the NG Kerk. Every holiday, we'd dread the invasion of the Vaalies (from the then Transvaal) and *Vrystaaters* (from the then Orange Free State) making their pilgrimage to the coast for the school holidays. Natalians sported car stickers that said, "Vaalies, Go Home" and other, worse stuff despite the fact the domestic tourists supported the local tourism and were a major contributor to the economy. To us, they were Wingnuts, *Kydaars*, Rockspiders and *Fokin'* Dutchmen.

Occasionally, my sisters and I would have to bunk in with my brothers to make space for various black people, mainly ministers, who would come to stay with us during Synod or other church meetings, as there was no other accommodation for them. In those days, having a black person stay overnight in a white area was a crime, so it was all rather exciting for us.

Our life was weird and tense. Dad seemed increasingly frustrated at the lax stand the Anglican Church was making against apartheid, and his sermons were sometimes carefully peppered with anti-government innuendos. Mum, on the other hand, had befriended a couple of policemen and on occasion we'd go for joy rides in police cars with sirens wailing.

Our mother was more hung up on class distinction than race. There was nothing worse than being 'common'. Rudeness was common, she said. So as kids, she always made us wait for a black person in front of us at the café to be served first – no queue jumping because of our skin colour. And we could never refer to a black man or woman as 'the girl' or 'the boy' as it would get us a clip round the ear and a stern lecture on 'respect for elders'.

Of course there were white people I was aware of who were opposed to the apartheid government, and I was especially impressed with women like Helen Suzman and the Progressive Party, the Black Sash and Sheila Duncan, and Ruth First. I vaguely remember sadness in our home during the 1976 student uprising and the murder of Steve Biko in 1977. But shielded exposure to an apartheid system blunted my abhorrence of a system of which I had very little knowledge. I didn't know any black or Indian children of my age because we lived in separate worlds and it was really incredibly weird and confusing.

We never spoke about politics in our home. Dad would sometimes pass a few bitter remarks during the SABC radio news on Radio Port Natal, and Mum would look increasingly strained. At school, we'd hear silly tales of how 'the girl' always stole food and clothes and stuff, enjoyed endless streams of unsavoury boyfriends in and off properties, how the phone calls were always for 'the girl', and how 'they' never lifted a finger but spent their lives hanging over fences chatting to all the other mammas in the neighbourhood. When I visited friends, I was startled to find that domestic helpers always had their own cupboard with a tin plate, cup and cutlery because of their black-person germs. It seemed odd that for many those hands were good enough to handwash your panties, wash your dishes and make the bed – but heaven forbid they touch the same mug. Or that they were not allowed to use the inside toilet. Even as a child, I was embarrassed when teachers told us to leave our unwanted sandwiches, sometimes squashed or with a bite or two missing, in a special bag for the cleaners, who were supposed to have been grateful for our leftovers.

Naturally, our education was biased towards supporting the apartheid myth and the history was so slanted it now seems bizarre we accepted it. This was probably an indictment on the education system, which then consisted of teachers speaking only and us learning from hand-outs rather than the modern style of students doing their own research for projects.

Our evenings were spent either playing cards or playing Scrabble, reading books, and listening to our parents' LPs on my grandmother's hand-me-down gramophone.

Friday afternoons we'd go to the local library and be allowed to choose three books each, then Friday night our treat was to huddle around the radio and listen to our favourite Springbok Radio show, *Squad Cars*. All five kids would chant along to the opening prologue.

But we also loved *Taxi*, the Springbok Top 20 with David Gresham ("Keep your feet on the ground and reach for the stars") and the quiz show *Check Your Mate* and my older brother loved *The Mind of Tracy Dark* and *My Name is Adam Kane*, too weird and scary for the rest of us. We spent most of our holidays at the beach in Durban, a 20-minute car drive from Pinetown, where we would smear ourselves in oil and fry our skins brown. White skins trying to go brown, brown-skinned people bleaching themselves to go white – yes, they were crazy times indeed.

Then in 1976, my first year in high school, we got our first television. It was only a black-and-white set, but those two hours of screening time each evening were thrilling. *Biltong and Potroast*, *Shane* ("Shane, Shane, I love you, Shane"), *The Brady Bunch* (I still know the words to the song), *The Dingleys* with the theme tune by Rabbitt, and *The Villagers* about a mining community.

But it wasn't comfortable being a white English-speaking girl growing up in South Africa. I didn't fit.

Secretly, I envied the Indians, with their flashy homes, zooty cars, fabulous clothes and bright jangly jewellery. The schoolgirls got to wear these pristine white uniforms and they had a sense of unity. I longed to belong somewhere. Like Africans, as black people were called then, South African Indians had a cause. They had a history and sense of themselves; they were a proper community with culture and a sense of who they were. Plus Mahatma Gandhi was one of them, someone I hugely admired, before I read somewhere that he beat his wife.

I also wanted to be Jewish for the same reason I wanted to be Indian, to be part of a larger community, to have a sense of belonging.

By the time I reached my teens, hormones kicked in and I was flooded with an enormous hunger for adventure, independence and freedom. I was torn between two basic and desperate desires – clinging to my family and breaking free.

My general frustration with apartheid only added to my adolescent confusion. Of course, having a government I could only despise fuelled my life-long distaste for authority. I'd write childish history essays condemning the homeland policy, referring to the homelands as "dumping grounds for unwanted Africans". And I once made a school speech about South African leaders – "somewhere, someplace, in a kraal, prison or homeland somewhere lies one who is destined to become the pioneer of the future to come – but will he or she be in time?" Needless to say, I wasn't put forward to represent my school at the next round of the competition.

I struggled with school. I was bored and hated having to sit copying down notes without being able to question the relevance of the information. Looking back at the set history book – our history involved the glorification of Boers and their struggle against nature, natives and the British, and the only mention of black history was where Hertzog, Smuts and Malan dealt with 'the Native Problem' or 'the Native Question'. Ours was a world where events happened with no explanation.

I felt trapped by my youth and school and longed for the freedom to control my destiny, where I could fly away to an exciting life filled with activity. I wanted to be my own story. Looking back now, maybe it's a case of being careful what you wish for in case you get it.

My parents divorced when I was 17 years old and my dad remarried. He left the ministry and went off to lecture at the University of Natal (Pietermaritzburg), where he later went on to briefly become a Deputy Vice-Chancellor. Andrew was already at university there, so Simon, Catherine and I headed off to live with my dad on campus in a massive double-storey house. Lucy went to Durban with my mother, joining us at varsity in 'Maritzburg a few years later. Because studies were free, we all attended the University of Natal as students, even my dad's wife Gail, and we hung together in a close-knit family pack. I completed a BA degree, majoring in English and Religious Studies, but was not a very committed student. I simply wanted the degree – a very useful piece of paper in the job market, no matter what people tell you – and I passed all subjects with the narrowest of margins. As for university politics, I tried to join a few liberal causes and anti-apartheid groups on the campus but I disliked the mossy-bottomed muesli-eating pinkoes who were too intelligent and academic for a lightweight airhead like me. But I had even less in common with the influx of the crazy Zimbo contingent fresh from the Rhodesian War who drank out of their *veldskoene*, defecated in their rooms and slept in tents outside the residence halls. Nor was I keen on the white sons of Zambian farmers who chanted, "One Zambia, One Nation, One Kaffir Creation." I was shocked by the youngsters who thought it funny to get drunk and drive around throwing beer cans and glass bottles out the windows at blacks walking on pavements. So I mainly hung out with Andrew and Catherine where we'd spend Saturdays in the Polo Tavern drinking warm box wine and Castle Lager.

I genuinely felt there was little a young white woman could do to make a difference without being patronising – so I verbally abused the government at every opportunity and waited for the change I never doubted had to come.

By the end of my university days, I graduated with the degree and a fiancé, Pete W, a lanky man with heart-melting toffee eyes and a gentle, laid-back personality. We moved to Johannesburg and built a house, shared a 'child' – a beloved border collie called Barry – and I flittered about trying to find my groove. At that time, I even aspired to being a spoilt princess, to driving a fancy cabriolet, enjoying long lunches and drinking fruity but deadly cocktails. It took some time before I decided to knuckle down and find a career direction.

I had started thinking about being a journalist when I was about 10 years old. I won R5 in a *Sunday Times* writing competition in the Children's Club section. When I was younger, I thought I might want to be a Christian missionary despite not believing Jesus was the son of God. Then I vaguely romanced the idea of being a truck driver. Of course, I now realise that I merely wanted to travel and have adventures. Since I am interested in many things for a short time with something new every day, newspaper journalism seemed to perfectly suit my personality.

So I got off my lazy ass and took action. Off I went to beg for a job at a local knock-and-drop outfit before trying to get a job on the country's biggest-selling daily newspaper, *The Star*. The editor told me to get a job at the smaller daily newspaper, *The Citizen*, for experience.

My problem with *The Citizen* was that it was alleged to have been secretly subsidised by the National Party government as an alternative to the *Rand Daily Mail* and *The Star* who were constantly criticising the government. So despite rather fancying myself as a left-wing anti-apartheid supporter, I accepted a job on a newspaper with a hugely charismatic editor, Johnny Johnson.

In my interview, he threw my portfolio aside, saying it was of no interest to him because good subbing could make even useless journalists look good.

"You can have the job," he said. "We need a good pair of tits in the newsroom."

I was sold!

He was a legend and truly fabulous. I adored his crazy work persona – white shirtsleeves rolled up, there first thing in the morning until after midnight day in and day out, and his completely un-PC newsroom management style. These were heady and exciting days indeed. The Doornfontein newsroom was always filled with passion and excitement, driven by a man who truly lived and breathed news. Many a dustbin went flying, people were fired on the spot, with Johnny shouting obscenities and stomping about.

Once I saw him actually rip up copy, stuff it in his mouth, chew it and then spit it out in disgust.

"This is bloody rubbish," he shouted.

It was all too fabulous.

"I started out as a copy runner when I was 15 years old – I had to lie about my age – and I worked my way up," he often told me.

He'd also pull me into his office and show me poetry he wrote, but I was too nervous to read it properly, so I just skimmed and hoped he'd never ask me to give my opinion.

I had insufficient idea of how to write a news story properly and Johnny was generous with his time and spot on with his advice to me, as he was to the many journalists who started their careers at *The Citizen*. Always calmly in the background was his unflappable wife, Cecily – the only person patient enough to be his secretary – who arrived every morning with a neat basket with floral lining containing Johnny's breakfast, lunch and dinner.

In those days, we wrote on word processors; everything was subbed manually and then pages were sent down a chute to the print room below. I basically learnt to report news, and discovered that no matter how much alcohol journalists drank during and after work, I was unable to acquire a taste for it!

Ironically, during my employment at *The Citizen*, my dad and his wife, Gail, made the news when they were arrested by police while protesting against the university quota system, which tried to limit the number of black students allowed to study at traditionally white universities. I read about it on the news feed at work and saw pictures of them being bundled into the back of a police van – before my brothers phoned to say they were going down to the police station to bail them out. Johnny was very kind and supportive that evening.

Covering the last whites-only election for *The Citizen* proved too much for me. I was so ashamed to be working for the newspaper, I couldn't go to work. So after a week, I got a letter from Johnny in the post.

"If you do not report to work in the next two days, we will consider your employment terminated."

I turned up the next morning and no further mention was made of my disappearance.

Despite the paper's compromised origins, I personally never saw my stories changed to suit a political agenda, nor was I aware of any blatant bias towards the ruling white National Party in my time there.

"We are a paper of record," Johnny always said proudly. And the newspaper was certainly packed with news at the expense of design.

But then – poised between apartheid and democracy – times were a-changing everywhere.

It was with a sad heart I said goodbye to *The Citizen* after one incredible year. It was only meant as a stepping stone to *The*

Star and part of me was still hugely mortified to be working for a newspaper that many deemed to be right-wing.

I applied once again to *The Star*, the best newspaper in Africa at that time. After a lengthy day-long interview and selection process, *The Star* gave me a job.

Chapter 3

Our wedding day in March 1991 was wedged between a trip to Israel during the Gulf War and the start of the pre-election violence.

A few weeks before our wedding, Ken and I went to Israel, holidaying with a group of Zionist Jews in the war zone. We went partly on a holiday, partly freelancing, because flights and accommodation were so cheap and we couldn't resist the excitement of experiencing war in another country.

We arrived to a stench of long-range rockets dropping out of the night sky onto Tel Aviv, US anti-missile Patriots, gas masks, sealed rooms and national fear.

It was the threat of chemical warfare that made the situation so unusual for us. Iraq and Saddam Hussein had already invaded Kuwait and were now raining Russian-made scud missiles down on Israel. For the first time in Israel's history, the country was under threat of serious destruction. The rumour was that Hussein would equip the missiles with chemical warheads.

As we landed at Ben Gurion Airport, every passenger was handed a cardboard handbag – a chemical and biological warfare kit – which included a gas mask plus injections filled with liquid to dehydrate your entire body in case of a nerve gas attack. We were told that if a certain siren rang – long, without breaks – we were to plunge the injection through our clothing into our upper thigh, before making our way quickly to the nearest hospital for rehydration.

"I don't know if I could inject myself," I said.

"Don't worry," Ken replied, "I'll do you first."

The survival packs had become fashion accessories, with kids decorating theirs with colourful patterns or anti-Hussein graffiti. Others used them as handbags, throwing in their make-up, purses and other bits and pieces.

Of the 38 scuds shot at Israel in 19 attacks, none contained chemical weapons. Thousands of homes, apartments, shops and public buildings were destroyed. While only two civilians died in actual attacks, there were seven deaths from incorrect use of the warfare kits, and 225 serious injuries for those who received unnecessary injections of atropine.

When sirens wailed, we'd throw on our gas masks and head off to shelters where doors and windows were firmly sealed with tape to stop gas entering. Men would sit there reading newspapers with reading glasses over their masks, and the women would look after the little ones, many of whom were crying in bewilderment or fear. One Ethiopian family, who arrived in Israel the week the scuds started dropping, remained in their room wearing gas masks for eight hours because they didn't understand the Hebrew commands on the radio. Sometimes, Ken and I wouldn't bother to join everyone and stayed in our room with our gas masks on depending on what we were up to.

It was only after Ken died that I found this poignant love note, written while we were staying at the Jerusalem Gate Hotel.

"A moment of passion and love – destroyed by war 23/01/91.

"The moon rising, sirens around us, the hostile hint, grim realisation as speakers blurb a Hebrew Emergency order: 'Air Raid, put on your gas mask and move to the sealed rooms immediately.' We laugh but there is no joy. There is no happiness in the parting caused by war."

The most fun was watching the international media operating, since we were both still really young and inexperienced. These media entourages had mega-money as it was still at a time when newspapers and magazines spent big on overseas assignments. They'd set up cameras on roofs of hotels and simply wait. But one night, when a missile struck a kindergarten in a Tel Aviv suburb, the media jumped into their hired cars and charged off. We merely called a taxi whose driver, using a radio connecting him to others in the city, took us right to the scene before the rest of the media caught up with us. It was all about the race for me ... getting there first!

We were travelling with a delightfully earnest group of young Zionist men showing their support and solidarity to Israel as a Jewish state. For Ken and me, it was a weird and fascinating pre-marriage 'holiday' – war tourism – where we went simply to be part of history.

The day we left, I visited the Wailing Wall in Jerusalem, a sacred site in the old City of Jerusalem built by Herod the Great in 4BC. With its huge limestone walls stained with tears from many millions of crying souls, many believe this the place to get the 'ear of God'. I put my prayer into the crack of the ancient wall.

"Please God, give me a long and happy marriage to Ken. Fill my life with love and adventure. And don't let me ever get fat."

As for Ken, this was his last diary entry on our flight back home – the last as a single man.

"Getting married to Monica in two weeks. The beginning of a new era all over again. Life just heaves and bumps and rolls on and on, away."

The night before we married, I made this diary entry.

"I am now totally committed to living the rest of my life with him – just wish I hadn't missed out so much of HIS life – and it's quite scary loving someone so deeply. I am really excited about getting married ... not the ceremony as I hate organised shit – but knowing my life is changing for the better."

His reply?

"How's my tough soft-as-silk woman?

"It's a mad world ... innit? But through the haze there is a reason and love and laughter ... and I just wanted to tell you I love you and how kif it is to come home and know you'll always be here ... that's what.

"Cheers for now … and in this sad world, be happy.
"love u"

Ken organised most of the wedding – from invites to catering – as entertainment is just not my thing at all. I am too lazy to bother and seriously would have been happy to simply invite everyone to our home, order in pizza and a few boxes of wine and beer.

We did have a bit of a mishap the night before while trying on rings to make sure they fitted. Ken got his on, and then couldn't get it off again. Poor love nearly ripped his finger off in panic.

We started off with a civil ceremony at the place where we first locked eyes – in the Randburg Magistrate's court – with just our immediate families. It was a simple affair where we wore jeans and T-shirts, kissed like teenagers and introduced families.

The next day, we had a wedding at his father's farm in Knoppieslaagte between Johannesburg and Pretoria. It didn't just rain; it bucketed down. Our wedding was slap bang in the middle of the wettest few days recorded in Johannesburg for 45 years. It rained so long and so hard, the parking area soon became a deep muddy bog where many guests – well, the ones who found the place – got stuck. Ken wore a dodgy suit he'd bought at a midnight sale at some downtown Johannesburg outfitters, and I was dressed in the shortest mini dress ever. It was meant to be a prim top-and-skirt affair but I laughed off the skirt and simply added a pair of cream stilettoes, sexy stockings and frilly panties. I didn't even remember the traditional bouquet of flowers.

"Stop," I said to my brother en-route to the wedding.

Jumping out the car, I hopped over the fence of a home with a front garden and stole a bunch of yellow Christmas daisies, in my micro-mini and cream stilettoes in the pouring rain. So classy.

But as I walked into the marquee and saw Ken's soulful face looking across at me, my heart was full. I felt not one bit of doubt, no fear whatsoever – and marriage seemed like a momentous occasion. Ken took it all very seriously, whereas I was simply happy being the centre of attention. But when he spoke his vows with such heartfelt commitment, tears rolled down my cheeks.

Our guests were an eclectic mix of old friends, family and

people from work we liked or wanted to know better. My family, of course, are used to me – but I am not sure his family or some work colleagues were very impressed with my 'dress', which caused a few tight lips and not a few tut-tuts. After the ceremony, I cartwheeled in the rain, flashing my panties and throwing my arms into the air. Our pictures included umbrellas, flying mud and jubilant scenes of wedded bliss.

We honeymooned at the same Eastern Transvaal game reserve where we'd fallen in love the year before.

We were not a popular couple and I know people liked to mock us behind our backs because we were such easy targets. I now also cringe at some memories of us too. Ken was rather brash and prickly, with an awkward manner that came across as pompous and arrogant. I, on the other hand, was loudly showy, too outspoken and insensitive – all nah-nah perky and me-me-me. So our wedding was a perfect opportunity for people to have a snigger. Wedding pictures pinned on the noticeboard in the photographic department were defaced with vulgar and unkind comments. And many in the newsroom placed bets on how long our marriage would last.

We tried not to care.

"We have created our reality by allowing ourselves to come together and committing one another to the other," Ken wrote to me. *"There is the reality of everything around us which has always been there, but we have to create our own shared reality within all this. And the only thing that it is, and can be, based on is love, and I love you; that is beyond my control."*

We were joined at the hip. We lived and worked together – albeit different shifts sometimes – but we were seldom apart.

One of the first times Ken and I were separated was when he was sent to India to cover South Africa's return to the international sporting scene – the South African cricket team versus the Indian team. I felt physically ill at our parting and pined for him to the point of nausea. And he would either phone or fax me as often as he could – at least every day.

Letter from The Oberoi Grand in Calcutta (now Kolkata) India – 11/11/91:

"I wish I could say I am having a great time – this place is wonderful but I'm just too fuckin' tired and brain dead too tired – my arms are falling off … so tired I can't drive my pen … to shoot this place I need months – incredible – but a stinking mass of humanity – and traders rob you blind … I love you and wish you were here and see what could be with time and nose filters …"

On another occasion, he headed off to Zimbabwe to do a story on the tobacco industry – and once again, being apart was horribly difficult. I got this lonely little fax on the second night away after he couldn't reach me by phone.

"Monica, you seem so far away. I don't want you to come into this fucked-up environment. I've got to get through to you sharp – I wish you were here, but not HERE!"

And while many of Ken's 'friends' came pouring out the woodwork years later, in the time we were married many were quite nasty to him. Ken's World Press Photo entries 'accidentally' went unposted one year, another photographer bad-mouthed Ken to get a freelance gig at a major US news magazine, there was endless petty sniping in the photographic department and no one missed an opportunity to make his life uncomfortable. It was not helped by the fact that Ken presented himself as being egotistical and pushy to counteract his inferiority complex. Highly self-critical, he held himself up to high standards and was deeply ashamed of revealing any weakness or insecurity in public.

When he was made Chief Photographer at *The Star*, many staff photographers bristled at Ken's enthusiastic visions for the department and spent time sneering at his efforts to lead by example. It made me furious. He was also under pressure to conform to management's conservative style, difficult for an idealistic young man with zealous ideas on photography. And when he got hurt – which he did, being really very sensitive underneath his hot-headed bravado – I'd leave him supportive notes.

"It makes me furious when people call you arrogant. Don't change for anyone and never become a grovelling simpering yes man. Don't let the Star *turn you into a little grey man and part of their giant system. I love the way you are … let's take life less*

seriously – our life is too short to get bogged down by trivia and petty problems – especially at work – so have a lekker day – be you and have fun doing it ..."

Ken expected others to love working as much as he did, when in fact there were loads of laid-back photographers who saw pictures as only a job and were resentful of Ken's incredible work ethic. So I'd urge him to stand firm.

"Speak out. Be strong and stick to your principles. Don't let the other photographers bullshit you into accepting their norm. Whatever you say, think or do, I'm right there supporting you. I appreciate you for your many, many talents so don't let anyone undermine you or your confidence – you're the best and I love you."

I was more confident at work, albeit it was probably misguided. It certainly helped that I worked on the crime desk where sensational stories write themselves, so talented subbing and front-page stories made me look good. But I also had Ken to guide me, put me in the right place at the right time, and illustrate my copy with his excellent photographs.

Life with Ken was filled with romance and loving gestures. Books, magazines, perfume, lotions and creams ... every week there was something.

One day, I came home from work to find an envelope with keys.

"To our new home."

The previous week, we'd driven past the house and I mentioned how it would be good to buy one day.

"One day ..." I wished.

Next week there it was – an envelope with keys to our new home – a tiny two-bedroom home in a housing estate in Randpark Ridge, Extension 47. It probably says something that he made such a big purchase without consulting me – but to me, it was a beautiful gift. The day we moved in, he filled our house with flowers and carried me over the threshold. We put on music and danced in the living room, on the furniture and up and down the tiny passage to the bedroom into the night.

1992: Ken to Monica

"Without all or any of the niceties or heart-graphics I want to

put myself in context in your life. I love you. Being your husband is the most important thing in my life. It means I have committed myself to you for life. Now that's going to take a long time – the longer the better.

"It means that I want to be in your company, hold or receive your love because that's obviously a driving force in my life. It means that I have trust and confidence in you. It can be just everything I dreamt of.

"I love you, like you, want you, need you, desire you and I am coming home to GET you!

"You make me see love, feel love, feel perfect and I hope I do something for you. I do try!"

But our life wasn't all pink roses and passion. Our relationship was set against a background of political turmoil, violence and tragedy as South Africa made the transition between an apartheid regime and a genuine free and fair democracy for all.

Chapter 4

Ours was a love in dramatic times. Romance whirled and swirled against the background of an extraordinary chapter being written in South African history. Poised on the brink of enormous change, Ken and I were privileged to report on the end of the dark apartheid years and the start of an era where all South Africans could vote, irrespective of colour.

My job at *The Star* began with the unbanning of political parties and the end of the State of Emergency in February of 1990. In his speech at the opening of Parliament, the then president of South Africa, FW de Klerk, announced the unbanning of the African National Congress (ANC) and other banned organisations, and the release of ANC leader Nelson Mandela after 27 years in prison.

Initially, we were all filled with euphoria as South Africa seemed to be on the brink of endless beautiful possibilities. Then the dark, ominous clouds blew in.

The township violence – focused on Natal and Johannesburg and surrounding townships like Soweto, Katlehong and Thokoza – took us all by surprise. One minute, we were all looking forward to a peaceful transition into democratic rule – and the next, thousands of people were being slaughtered.

At first, it appeared to be black-on-black violence – aggression between the Inkatha Freedom Party, led by Mangosuthu Buthelezi, and the African National Congress. As I understood it, Inkatha and Buthelezi had opted to cooperate with the National Party during the apartheid years in order to get a better ideal for Zulus in Natal. The African National Congress decided to go underground and fight. So when all the parties were unbanned, there was resentment and competition. Police were often seen siding with warring Inkatha warriors during internecine clashes, using force against marauding ANC mobs, which further exacerbated disorder. Plus, police were being connected to the murky Third Force, which was out to destabilise the entire democratic process and prevent the ANC from gaining too much power. Throw into that cauldron of bubbling tension the right-wing factor – led by Eugène Terre'Blanche and others – and South Africa became a fertile breeding ground for bloody bedlam.

And so began an orgy of butchery and war – political wars, tribal wars, taxi wars – a veritable smorgasbord of violence and chaos. In the next four years, 14 000 people were killed and many more thousands injured, mostly in the homeland of KwaZulu and the neighbouring Natal province, and in the PWV (Pretoria–Witwatersrand–Vereeniging) region of the Transvaal.

It was an age of crisis and confrontation, a time of endless political rallies, marches and tense stand-offs. This was an era of necklacing, where a tyre placed around a person was doused in petrol and set alight. There were also slogans like "One settler, one bullet".

As turmoil reigned, political parties including the ANC and the National Party were meeting at the World Trade Centre in Kempton Park for the Convention for a Democratic South Africa (CODESA) to discuss the way forward in South Africa. The Conservative Party and the Pan African Congress initially didn't participate at all, and Inkatha had only nominal representation. During this time, national leader FW de Klerk held the 'whites-only' referendum where the majority of white South Africans voted to continue negotiations towards a free South Africa.

As negotiations ebbed and flowed, the violence ramped up during those four years – from the release of Nelson Mandela to him then becoming the first black president of South Africa.

Ethnic violence started in the Natal Midlands, which was an Inkatha stronghold. During Easter of 1990, Ken and I spent the weekend taking pictures and interviewing refugees hiding out in a church outside Pietermaritzburg after their menfolk were attacked and homes destroyed by Inkatha warlords. Our Monday-morning spread of front-page stories and pictures established Ken and me as a working couple – and we continued to work as often as possible as a team.

Not long after this, I went with Ken into a township near Vereeniging and there, sprawled on a dusty road, was a young boy, shot in the chest, a small plastic gun lying by his side. He tried to say something. Then he died. The youngster had been caught between warring factions and his toy gun mistaken for the real thing.

On another occasion, I was working the early-morning shift and a photographer (not Ken, who was home sleeping in) and I went out to cover a story of a woman who had been burnt to death in the veld outside Soweto. The woman had lain in the sun for a day or two before being discovered. Men from the morgue carefully slid a small stretcher underneath her body, but when they lifted it, her feet fell off. The photographer, who had just eaten a toasted egg-and-bacon sandwich, started retching. But I laughed. I could not stop giggling. Of course, it wasn't funny, just incredibly shocking.

During these years of bloody devastation, we were up before dawn, racing around townships counting the victims of the night's violence. One night, after attending an evening rally in Soweto, we unexpectedly came across an army of men creeping through the veld in Meadowlands, their eyes shining like cats' in the headlights of our car. Both thrilled and terrified, we let the car idle, trying to establish what was happening. Too afraid to get out of the car, we circled the area a few times, then lost sight of the men as they disappeared into the blackness. The next day, I read in the police report that ANC supporters had been slaughtered in the nearby Dube hostel after an attack by Inkatha vigilantes.

Our pictures and stories were filled with combatant parties wearing bandanas, brandishing machetes, iron bars and pangas. Parts of many townships became no-go zones and Casspirs patrolled by day with police dispersing crowds with teargas, water cannons and military force. Residents continued to report that police attacked them at night, setting fire to squatter camps, and that police were seen giving weapons to Inkatha.

Ken's most memorable image of the violence was taken on the first day he photographed township violence in the Transvaal. A terrified girl was pulling a younger child across the road as a menacing impi of Zulus armed with spears and pangas marched down Khumalo Street in Thokoza to attack a neighbouring hostel. Ken managed to capture the primeval force, the terrifying human machine of group hostility, in a photograph that stunned South Africans.

Thokoza was a derelict township about 16 kilometres south-west of Johannesburg where the main road – Khumalo Street – linked a number of migrant workers' hostels. Some housed mainly Inkatha supporters, and others were filled with ANC supporters – and those living alongside the road were caught in the crossfire. At first, journalists and photographers felt comfortable driving through there – but as the war heated up and the situation became increasingly hostile and unpredictable, it became a serious no-go zone.

This is Ken's diary entry the night of 22/08/1990:

"'Just another day, just another assignment,' I thought as we approached the sprawling East Rand township of Thokoza on a warm, sunny early spring day.

"'We hear there's some trouble brewing out there ... wanna take a look?' said pics editor David Sandison ... and so started the most testing week so far of my experience as a South African press photographer working in this weird, turbulent and twisted social menagerie we know as home.

"The road hummed with everyday bustle of township life; oversized women behind boxes packed with fruit and fresh vegetables, peanuts and shoelaces from the next trader trading on a blanket under the African sun, fifteen passengers waiting to cram

in the 'Zola Budd' taxi, knots of barefoot children twirling to get a foot to a dusty old tennis ball in their perpetual game of township soccer, the battered facade of a hostel blurred passed us on the right, peeling paintwork and shattered windows the trademark of these strife-torn abodes of urbanisation of the migrant work force.

"Then we saw them. Just up front. A group of about 100 men moving along the road into the township. But they were just the rear guard. Ahead of them a mass of men, bristling with weaponry, anonymous impi of blatant destruction. These are urban warriors of Inkatha, self-identifiable by their rag-tag red headbands of torn cloth, rope, plastic sacking and packing ... to taunt the bull.

"All I knew is that I had to get in front of them, give me time to look ... time to think ... time to work into them ... time and space to get out if naked hostility bore down. The driver of the car, Johannes, is nervous. 'Good, they're ignoring the car and marshalling the left side of the car.'

"The car clears so we speed ahead ... park, bump out and move into the road and watch as they come on down, chanting, waving their weapons of war, closer and closer ...

"Suddenly, a flash of movement to my right and its two young girls, the older one pulling the younger by a tightly clasped hand, running across the road in front of the advancing Zulus for the safety of their gate, and practically without thinking I pick up on them, focus and – zanga-sanga-sanga-sanga – four frames shot to start the day's work. Unaware that I'd just shot my most telling image of the day, I move left and go down on one knee, camera braced resting on the other, already changed to a wide lens to get the front-rankers towering over the viewer, to get the children's perception of the impi bearing down ... it's all pictures now, reality takes a back seat, replaced by the immediacy of the image. If the picture can't tell the story, what will?

"Bigger and bigger they grow, storming up to fill the frame, and just as I'm about to let rip and shoot, the front rank and then the ranks swarming passed me, stop. In their tracks. And proudly brandish their weapons, waving and shaking crude assegais and hand-carved kieries, formidable chunks of steel piping and *home-made axes, the odd genuine cowhide shield strangely inappropriate. I shoot a few frames and hold my ground, and the army gets impatient and resumes its march, swallowing me up. A few more frames and I stand up, turning, to become one with the impi, a chanting and dancing mass of men with a mission ... and down the road we march, the infectious rhythmic motion carrying me along, looking left and looking right, taking in the faces and the fury of these men – a hot undercurrent of hatred gearing down in a headlong rush through the suburb. Young men, strong men, working men, men carrying age-worn kieries and young bucks leaping and swinging honed spears and kieries, after their kill.*

"Problems, photographic problems. How to hone in on this swaying mass to display the weaponry, the intent, the size of the band on the run? Go wide, 24 mil held above my head, turning to run backwards holding the pace and staring into the faces of the Zulu closest to me, bang off a few frames and turn back into the flow of direction, changing pace to drop through into another portion of the mass, new faces, new pangas, new knives and blades, two-sided axes behind shields real and cardboard.

"And still the rhythm of the march, onwards to an uncertain destination. On passing an empty soccer field with the chanting multitude of voices ringing their battle cry in my ears 'Usuthu ... Usuthu', I feel the battle but I know not where and wonder how I'll move now to shoot when we engage the enemy. I felt the fight coming on, I didn't know why or where or even who this war was against, but the anti-Mandela theme soon came through in song, if you can call it that; a rolling rhythm of scorn heaped on an unseen adversary. Anger was piling in and being nurtured in the bosom of this living beast.

"And suddenly we stop, hemmed closed up in front by a bevy of police iron; an immovable front of hulking camouflaged Casspir, a few 'yellow perils' and a yellow police bus disgorging clad riot figures with their paraphernalia of weapons and real-real bullet throwers. I shoot easily over the top of the mass of a cop eyeing out the impi from the privileged position of the door of the bus. I shoot some police brass vaguely evident through the web of spiky

weapons texturing the crowd. An angry militancy exudes vocally from a swarm of front rankers but the dialogue is too distant for me to pick it up. A brief negotiation and the impi surges forward again, now with an escort of police. Ushered on down the road."

That night, when his kombi pulled up late at home and he didn't come inside immediately, I went out and saw him slumped over the steering wheel, lying on his arms.

"You okay?" I asked.

"I'm not sure," he replied. "I don't really think so."

A few months later, Ken was caught up in one of the most horrifying experiences of his life. He photographed marauding Inkatha warriors going from hostel to hostel in Vosloorus, breaking down doors and attacking dwellers with pangas and machetes, killing hostel dwellers believed not to be IFP supporters. Ken had been allowed – even encouraged – to take pictures. He saw first-hand the build-up to the attack, the singing and the rising bloodlust.

He was particularly stunned at the reaction of the hunted.

"They just whimpered or froze with terror, like rabbits caught in headlights," Ken told me.

"It was so eerie – no screaming, no running, like the victims were paralysed with fear.

"I just heard the blunt sound of hacking – and when I went in the room afterwards, there was another body just lying there," he said.

Every week our newspapers were filled with mass murders and mob killings. We covered endless stories of the death tolls and horrific injuries, shacks set alight and dwellers burnt, families left homeless, refugees standing with only the clothes they were wearing. We tried to capture their despair and their fear. We even interviewed first-year school children in the Alexandra township who had leapt out of windows and been injured because a group of Inkatha men wearing red headbands and bristling axes and knobkerries had marched through their school. The children thought they were about to be massacred.

Once I saw a man dead in his neat shack, his genitals mutilated, with his tea and sandwich sitting neatly on the makeshift table.

Another time, a man was shot dead sitting on the toilet. Always bodies and grieving relatives, distress and uncertainty, frightened children and abandoned pets. Nowhere felt safe.

The violence ramped up and pangas and *knobkerries* were replaced with bombs, guns and automatic rifles. AK-47s and Molotov cocktails became fashionable. Shops were smashed open and looted during political marches through towns. Train violence became a terrifying reality. Men armed with automatic weapons would storm through the carriages, shooting passengers indiscriminately. Bricks and rocks were hurled in through windows as trains passed. Panic was so extreme that sometimes passengers would throw themselves out of the train windows onto the track – often to their death – if the call went up that the train was under attack.

One of our more bizarre assignments took place in the small town of Ventersdorp, home to right-wing leader of the *Afrikaner Weerstandsbeweging* (AWB) Eugène Terre'Blanche. A clash was brewing between about 300 militant AWB men who had been patrolling the town against the makeshift army of hundreds of residents gathered in the neighbouring Tsing township. Both sides were armed with an assortment of weapons – sticks, guns, clubs, axes, pangas and knives. It all started when farmers beat up squatters living on a nearby farm and burnt down their homes. White residents allegedly then received telephone calls threatening that township dwellers planned to murder them and burn down their houses. Terre'Blanche retaliated with threats of doing anything to protect his volk, including killing squatters if he had to. After attending a right-wing rally in the town, Ken and I went with a group of Tsing township dwellers to listen to their side of the story. Unfortunately, it was now dark and Ken and I were taken deep into the area before we were surrounded by a large group of agitated men. The situation started to get tense as some demanded to know why we were 'spying' on them. More and more people with a fierce assortment of weaponry started to gather tightly around us, barring any form of escape in the car, and we were ordered to get out and 'state our case'. It took a few calm residents and lots of negotiation for us to be guided out of the township – and I shook and giggled hysterically all the way back to the local Ventersdorp pub, where I planned to file copy. Suddenly, a fresh-faced young man fully decked in AWB insignia appeared in front of us, brandishing a pen knife.

"*Hou net aan*," he said. (Just hold on.) "You are under arrest."

He herded us off to a room off the bar.

"Wait here, I am going to call *Die Leier*."

And he left, locking the door behind him.

We climbed out the window, leapt into our car and headed straight back to the safety of Johannesburg.

Months later, while attending a packed Soweto stadium during Nelson Mandela's pre-election campaign trail, I felt my back burning. A youngster with a lighter was trying to set fire to my waist-length hair! Fortunately someone patted it out before more of my head went up in flames. The damage was nothing a hair trim and new T-shirt couldn't fix. I later heard it had happened to another long-haired journalist as well.

The shocking story of a group of misguided white Afrikaner right-wingers on a '*kaffirskiet piekniek*' in Bophuthatswana still horrifies me. Bophuthatswana was one of four homelands that accepted nominal independence from Pretoria, but under the new South Africa these homelands would once again fall under South African rule. President of Bophuthatswana, Lucas Mangope, refused to allow the ANC to campaign and called on the right-wing Conservative Party leader, Constand Viljoen, to assist his Bophuthatswana Defence Force (BDF) in repelling the ANC. However, the poorly disciplined AWB decided to join in and drove in, shooting people as they passed small towns. But the BDF turned on them and opened fire on one group of AWB men. As these three white men lay injured and bleeding into the dust, a flock of media stood by and interviewed them. Suddenly, a local soldier opened fire on the injured men in front of television cameras, massacring them. At the time, I was strangely accepting of these chilling deaths. The AWB, though small in number, had been responsible for many acts of terror, killing and injuring dozens of children and innocent people in attacks on squatter camps, and bombs placed in taxi ranks and bus stops.

"Serves them right, bloody idiots," I said. "Better them dead than let them loose to kill defenceless bystanders."

I felt really annoyed that Ken had been so profoundly shaken because I saw it as a sign of being weak and unprofessional. I didn't want him to feel sorry for right-wingers associated with an organisation that attacked and had killed innocent black people. Although he was at the scene, he missed the actual shooting, so a lot of his initial attention was focused on being furiously disappointed he missed the action photographs. But the image of the men pleading for their lives before being shot really upset Ken.

One of the bloodiest and most brutal moments in the lead-up to elections was the Boipatong massacre outside Vereeniging where more than 45 people were killed on the night of 17 June 1992. Township residents told reporters that police had played a role in the Wednesday-night massacre, along with Zulu-speaking migrant workers from the Inkatha Freedom Party.

Shortly after this, on 7 September of the same year, the Ciskei Defence Force, under command of military leader Brigadier Oupa Gqoza, opened fire on 80 000 ANC supporters opposing his rule, killing 28 marchers and one soldier in Bisho (now Bhisho).

Then, not five months later, 19 IFP warriors were shot and killed outside the ANC stronghold in Johannesburg, Shell House, after the IFP threatened to attack.

On Easter Friday in April 1994 Ken was in Durban covering the increased violence in squatter camps set deep in the lush green hillsides outside the city. As we were watching a group of women praying, snipers across the road opened fire and a woman was killed and a few were badly injured. I found her three young children cowering in a makeshift hut. When I asked a neighbour who would now care for these little ones, she shrugged her shoulders. Deadlines loomed so copy had to be filed, then I had a family lunch to attend, and life moved on. I'd wake at night with a tightness in my throat.

The tragedies also included the breakdown of society and the consequences of overladen government welfare services. I shed many tears on a story of three primary-school brothers who'd run away from home. On being discovered hiding in the bush in a storm-water drain, the children sobbed and begged not to be returned to their mother. The older brother said the mother's boyfriend had been raping them. The State sent the boys back because there was nowhere else for them to go. I spent a day on the phone, calling welfare departments, police liaison officers and child protection services – and the answer was always the same: "Everywhere is full". The reasoning was that the boyfriend was no longer living with the mother and the boys were going to be sent to a boarding school, so would only be at home during the holidays.

So many massacres, and in between were endless raids on hostel dwellers, looting and burning, killing and maiming. Day in and day out, our papers were full of atrocious news and increasingly graphic images of death.

Chapter 5

No journalist or photographer liked to work alone in townships. Due to the clandestine operations by the police, the media couldn't depend on the SAP for reliable information. So a small group of photographers went into the townships at dawn to monitor any overnight action and count the dead before the morgue van arrived to collect the bodies.

"Come on, Mono Mon," Ken would say when the 5am alarm went off, "up and at it ... let's go."

In the cold winter mornings, we'd grab a cup of coffee to go, our hot breath fogging up the windows. I'd drive while Ken and Kevin hung out the open windows and took photographs. But I soon opted to cuddle back down in bed, so Ken started to join up with other photographers equally driven and ambitious.

Bang Bang – the sound of gunfire in the township – became the name of a group of photographers who regularly met for this morning dawn patrol, and this special group of friends were dubbed the Bang Bang Club by inspirational editor/keen photographer Chris Marais, in his *Living Africa* magazine. The main group were Ken, Kevin Carter, João Silva, Gary Bernard, American AP photographer Dave Brauchli, British freelancer Mike Persson and, later on, Greg Marinovich.

Initially, it was Ken and Kevin heading out on these dangerous missions, but after Ken and I got married, these two friends starting moving in different directions. Ken was far more balanced and emotionally calm, and he threw all his attention into his marriage and work, therefore adopting a much more conservative lifestyle. Kevin continued to be exuberantly disordered, bouncing from woman to woman and project to project. The 'brothers' were splitting into Good Twin and Naughty Twin. They continued working together but we seldom socialised with Kevin any more. I was definitely a wedge since they had already clashed over me a few times, initially because Kevin had fancied me, then because I consumed Ken's life. But despite the fact that their lifestyles were now increasingly divergent, they continued to have a special bond. Ken trusted Kevin implicitly, and they respected each other. Kevin remained a true friend always, one of the few Ken had in his life.

Then another personality was added to the scene – an unpretentious bundle of energy with the knack of befriending everyone with his down-to-earth and friendly personality.

"Who's that little Portuguese guy I checked you talking to in the photo department?" I asked Ken one day.

"João Silva," Ken said. "I want to give him a job. No real experience but he reminds me of me when I was starting out."

Ken never forgot how *The Star* photographic editors had once laughed at his portfolio when he was trying to get a job on newspapers, telling him that pictures of cute pets and kiddies were not going to crack it, and implying he was a lightweight blow-in. As a result of that humiliation, Ken always treated everyone interested in photography with a serious and generous spirit and offered advice, often spending time helping keen amateurs with guidance or inspiration. Ken loved João's passion and gumption, and as Chief Photographer at the time, successfully motivated for *The Star* to employ him.

In a letter addressed to the editor, Ron Anderson, in August 1991, Ken wrote:

"He (João) *is a tough, reliable and adaptable photographer capable of working across the spectrum of our society and his enthusiasm outweighs his relative inexperience … and he is the 'best buy' in town …"*

Although Ken and I didn't socialise much with anyone – too tired, too busy, too exclusive – Ken and João built a close working relationship and shared a real love for photo-journalism.

The international media rolled into town before elections and tried to latch onto Ken, Kevin and João because of their local experience and knowledge. Just riding into townships and finding their way around was a mission for foreigners, and the tight-knit Bang Bang Club huddled together to stop the foreign press from muscling in and taking over a scene they had been working on for years.

Ken was driven by the need to be the best photographer around – and to me and many others, he was by far the best. Ken used his image as photo-journalist to define himself and I was immensely proud of my husband and his work. Ken was able to capture moments of dramatic and poignant relevance – a single image interpreting an entire story. Often, his behind-the-scenes pictures of people – their actions and reactions, private moments of reflection captured by Ken from a distance – encapsulated the human picture behind the violence.

Ken might have been a tad gung-ho, but he was also a conservative and careful thinker. Only days before the elections, at a meeting planning *The Star*'s coverage of the election, he emphasised the need for less-experienced reporters and photographers to be protected. Working with me in the township was always stressful for him because he was driven to protect and look after me all the time, so he couldn't concentrate on his photographs. Conversely, when he was shooting, I carried his excess bags and covered his back. I also wasn't above elbowing people out of the way so he could get a better shot.

The non-stop workload with ever-increasing deadlines and the endless parade of death and destruction took its toll on journalists and photographers who worked during these times. We were all quite bonkers but we didn't realise how bizarre our lives were because we were so caught up in the drama. The incessant warring took its toll on all the media, no matter what colour or religion, and we were all affected in different ways by what we saw.

Ken's horror manifested itself in frightening dreams.

I woke one night, after Ken had been swept up in a particularly bloody massacre, to find him crying so hard his entire body was heaving.

I initially thought his body was cramping and having spasms.

"Just get up and stretch," I said.

It took time for me to realise he was whole-body sobbing. All I could do was hold him against me, soothing him like a baby, and wait for him to calm down.

We never spoke about that night or what caused him to be distressed – not ever again.

I, on the other hand, slept easily at night because I was always exhausted. But Ken continued having nightmares and sometimes woke me screaming. One night, he was hysterical but still asleep. Deeply frightened, I shook him and shouted.

"What's wrong? What's wrong?"

"It's a white rabbit … a white rabbit," he replied.

I burst out laughing and it became a long-running joke with us.

In his darkroom mid-1990:

"To: Darling Bunny Man.

"My darling intrepid Bunny Hunter You

"Panic – you half an hour late and newsroom freaking out. EEEK. You ok??"

And from Ken, a year later, when violence in townships was increasing, he sent me a fax from Durban where he was staying overnight.

"Seen any white rabbits lately? Seem to be dozens of them round my room."

Many photographers and journos drank heavily and smoked dope, and quite a few took increasingly hard-core drugs. Initially, it was just marijuana, mandrax and, for the real addicts, Welcanol. Then cocaine and crack became fashionable, with heroin creeping more and more into our world.

The night Kevin Carter won the Pulitzer Prize for his picture of a vulture watching a starving girl in a Sudanese camp was the first time I realised he was taking any drugs other than marijuana.

Colleagues who'd heard the news crowded into our lounge in a new house we had bought in 1994 in Randpark Ridge, round the corner from our first little house. Friends were trying to get hold of Kevin. But Kevin wasn't answering any calls. Ken and João went to find him at the place he was staying, to bring him to our home and help him front the flood of local and international media interest. *The New York Times*, for whom he took the winning picture, was desperate to make contact, and Kevin's friends were fielding the calls. As he staggered into our house, propped up by João and Ken, it was clear that Kevin was absolutely trashed. Grey-faced and incoherent, he stood swaying and sweating, confused, haggard and sick. He didn't seem to understand what was going on.

"What's *gaaning aan*? Whatchu saying?" he said. "Don't wanna talk to anyone … can't fucking talk to anyone."

His friends did the best they could to smooth the situation by helping Kevin through a call to *The New York Times*. When everyone went home and Kevin was eventually returned to his bed and tucked up, Ken and I were left in the lounge, shocked and upset by what we had just that night learnt about Kevin's serious drug problems.

Ken had the occasional alcoholic beverage – usually rum and ginger ale – but he was too busy working, getting pictures captioned and sent out to various agencies or to *The Star*. When he was away on assignments and staying in hotels, downtime was spent sleeping or eating. "It's preventative eating – eat now while you have a chance," he said.

On the rare day off he would come home and collapse on the couch.

While it was really difficult to remain unaffected by the violence, I felt it was impossible to have an emotional response to every death and every sad story.

"You are either a social worker or a journalist, but you can't be both," I often told myself and colleagues.

I was no different to the rest of the media.

When ambulances refused to go into townships during fighting to pick up badly injured people, the community sometimes looked to the journalists at the scene to help. Some of us paused, thinking of the hassle of blood on the seats and the risk of getting Aids.

"My job is to cover news and I can't be impartial if I start taking sides," I said.

I was not alone in this view.

Mainly, I was able to emotionally separate myself from the devastating effects of violence, death and grief. I also discovered that work was just one part of my life and, unlike Ken, I didn't want to spend all day every day chasing stories. I wanted to go to gym, or lie in the sun, drink coffee and read trashy airport best-sellers.

When Chris Hani, the leader of the SA Communist Party, was assassinated by right-wing fanatics in 1993, Ken phoned me from the office.

"Quickly, get into the newsroom," he said. "This story is big."

But it was Saturday and I was curled up on my bed with a book, again, and was simply too lazy to motivate myself to get excited.

I had become weary of the violence and it all began to blur into just another bloody day. I stopped being eager to cover many of these events and I no longer put my hand up to head out into the conflict areas. Somewhere over the years, I lost interest in hard news. It was too much effort. The continual story of fighting and dead bodies and confusion, with long hours, chasing about day and night, and constant work began to take its toll. It stopped being exciting or interesting for me. I wanted the freedom to adventure and explore and run free. Work was stifling me when I wanted to be having a good time.

So I escaped into my world of lightweight chick lit, and I slept a lot.

At the time, I thought I was perfectly okay, but looking back at some of my behaviour, I was clearly more aggressive than socially acceptable. In 1993, near our first home in Randfontein, a drunk driver and his friend spun their car and overturned while trying to do doughnuts on their way home from the local pub. When we heard the smashing and crashing, we ran out and found two men thrown from the car, bashed up and bleeding, with the contents of the car

45

strewn all over the road. One, dazed and frightened, asked Ken and me to phone his girlfriend. They were drunk. They said they had come from the pub, they stank of alcohol and the remains of brandy bottles were in the car. I was furious. Quivering with rage, I insisted that Ken didn't help them in any way. I stomped back home and fumed. In my mind, they were useless white trash who could have knocked over and killed the many children who played in the area.

Not long after, Ken and I were crawling home in rush-hour traffic over the Queen Elizabeth bridge in downtown Johannesburg when we saw a man smash and grab a necklace off a woman in the car behind us.

"What the fuck you doing?" I shouted as Ken jumped out the car to chase the guy and comfort the woman.

I was beside myself with fury. How could he delay our trip home over something so petty?

"Now I have to wait for you, and there is nowhere to pull over," I screamed.

So I just drove home and left him in the busy traffic, doing his good deed. He had to walk back to *The Star* and get a lift home with a journalist who lived near us.

On another occasion, when João Silva had an asthma attack while covering a story just outside *The Star*, I barely took time out to help him find an inhaler. There was a lot of shooting, with people hiding behind concrete bins to avoid flying bullets. João was running for pictures while battling to breathe – and then he started to panic. Yes, I did vaguely ask around for an inhaler. I did make the effort to tell picture editor Robin Comley about the problem. But I wasn't sympathetic. My view was that if he was sick and couldn't keep up, it was his problem, considering he smoked and had run outside without his inhaler.

"His problem, not mine," I thought.

In retrospect, this was very strange conduct\all round on my part; very odd indeed. When the going got tough, I became ultra-belligerent and self-justifying, then dived back into a book to block out the world again.

My fatigue and loss of enthusiasm were caused in part by my

confusion and discomfort about my role in reporting the violence. Sometimes township dwellers wrote letters to the newspapers condemning the white journalists – and especially the flood of international media – hanging around in the township hot spots. And their comments rang true.

"Go back to where you come from," a woman once yelled at me.

"You vulture ... you don't help us ... you make trouble," she shouted.

We followed the hot spots by tuning into police radio channels or listening to talk on the ground. Then the media pack prowled through townships like hyenas, waiting for an attack so we could move in and feast off the bloody news. We'd stroll around the dusty veld surrounded by litter and flies, watch factions posturing and brandishing weapons, hoping for action.

"Life's a bore when there's no war," was the popular slogan flung around by some of the photographers.

We only worked in the township for a few hours, feeding off the tragedy of others, and then left to go back to our newsrooms to file copy and then hang out in our lily-white suburbs telling boastful war stories of how close we came to being killed, thrilled by the terror, danger and drama.

I think of Ken's comment once that he worried that some killings felt staged for the media; that men were showing off for the cameras. Did we assist in monitoring and controlling a volatile political scenario, or did we merely fan the flames of violence? Were we recording history and showing the world other people's stories or were we just adrenalin junkies, selling sensation to the bloodthirsty reading public?

Our style of journalism was certainly in-your-face, with front-page pictures of dead bodies day after day after day. But then, if those who captured the conflict are held to account for doing so, perhaps the masses who consumed and demanded ever-more sensational images and stories might also be responsible.

Ken, along with a number of sub-editors, became worried about the constant demand both locally and abroad for the deluge of increasingly ghoulish images and stories.

In a diary entry in 1993, he wrote:

"There is happiness and beauty in South Africa and the photographs of this will come in time – maybe after freedom of the people has been achieved – but the world now demands the extremes in humanity and has conditioned photographers to move only the pictures."

Many of the white media had the vainglorious view that they were Knights in Shining Armour, fighting to record history to benefit The People. But with the passage of time to get our bizarre work into perspective, I think we had become both self-serving and desensitised to what was going on around us. I also bought into the pompous view of white journalists and photographers doing black South Africans a great service by showing the world the truth of what was going on.

While it is true that we were partly working in the townships because of our egos and entertainment, we were also trying to do the right thing. I also believe that overall we were doing meaningful work that has real value today. Looking back at South Africa's Truth and Reconciliation Commission's attempt to understand our past post the 1994 election, it was clear that we were vital in putting the story together. National Party bias in education and employment opportunities dictated that most local journalists were white, but that is not forgetting newsmen I worked with like Alf Kumalo, Walter Dladla, Juda Ngwenya and the delightful Jon Qwelane, Jovial Rantao and Mondli Makhanya. However, due to the consequences of apartheid, they were relatively few in number.

In retrospect, and with the benefit of maturity, I wish I had been more sensitive and less gung-ho, more in tune with the needs of the community as opposed to sensational front-page news. But under the circumstances, us whiteys did the best we could.

In some ways, being a white journalist and photographer had its benefits. At *The Star* newspaper, we had a system whereby we booked out a car, and a driver took us to the job and interpreted for us. In the early '90s, it seemed the white media were safer because the consequences would have been a lot more serious if someone killed a white person as opposed to a black person. Yes, I know, it's shocking, but that is the reality of how it was then, that white lives were treated by the media as more valuable.

In the end, though, I discovered that township violence didn't differentiate between skin colour.

Chapter 6

The first time Ken slapped me I thought my jaw had been dislocated. It was only bruised but the impact and shock left me stunned. We'd been dating less than eight months.

Ken and I had gone to a music festival in Swaziland and were travelling in Ken's kombi with a group of friends when we were stopped at a police roadblock and searched for drugs. A few grams of marijuana were found in one of the panels of Ken's van. So all six of us were arrested and chucked into holding cells while waiting to be let out on bail. However, because the amount of marijuana was so little, they wanted one person to take responsibility for it.

"Take responsibility for it, it's your car," I said.

In fact, it probably belonged to his older brother, an ex-prisoner with a then drug habit.

"No," he replied. "If we stand *vas*, they'll drop the charges," he reasoned.

I had to sit in a cell at the police station in Badfontein with other women until the police realised none of us in the van would claim the drugs. It was a waiting game that went on for a few hours. In the end, they charged no one and released us all with instructions to appear first thing on the Monday in the local magistrate's court. On the continued journey to Mbabane, I went on and on about his 'disgusting' family and his cowardly stance and how embarrassed I was.

"Pete wouldn't have let me be humiliated in that way," I said. "Obviously you don't love me enough."

When we got to the camp site, he threw me out the car and hit me so hard on the face, I fell to the floor clutching the place he'd hurt me, terrified. After about 20 seconds I stood up and dusted myself off. The others at the site, including Kevin and other male Johannesburg photographers just stood there, looking shocked and deeply uncomfortable, not sure whether to get involved or not. So I smiled shakily, took Ken's hand and walked away. Part of me sympathised with Ken. I had been so rude about his family and so irritating I would have been tempted to slap me myself. We walked about for a while in silence until we both calmed down and said sorry, but my jaw hurt for a day or two.

He smacked me often enough in our marriage for my jewellery box to be filled with single earrings. Somehow one always went flying somewhere and I either couldn't or didn't want to find it.

Sometimes I provoked the violence. I would push and push his buttons with my nagging and bitching and demands, wanting constant love and attention, forcing him to fit in with my way of thinking, and eventually he would snap and lash out.

Sometimes it was jealousy.

Once, he mistakenly thought a message left on the answering machine by the car mechanic about dropping off my car was an admirer coming to visit me. Before I knew what had happened, Ken stepped forward and smacked me so hard, I flew into the wall and hit my head.

On another occasion he thought I had been phoning my ex-boyfriend. He chased me out of the shower and out of the house with a knife. I sat naked in the back yard for a while until he'd calmed down and let me in again.

We fought about his lateness, his work hours, him sneaking off to visit his daughter, my neediness and my insecurities.

I was a complete bitch about his ex-girlfriend and the child they had together. Pathetically, I thought loving anyone else meant less love for me and I was a spiteful creature, something they all bore with rather more dignity than I would have. Before we got married, he understood it was me or his child – not both – but he had hoped once I felt more secure, I would be more accepting. By 1993, it was clear I was still relentless – and only having my own children 10 years later could make me understand what I was actually asking of him.

"Monica, there are people on the fringes who I have to have some consideration for even though they aren't central to my life, to our lives. I think I have shown you over the months that outsiders do not dominate or even form a significant part of our relationship. You are my reality, my friend, my companion, my lover and my wife. You are my future."

One minute I was incredibly warm, soft and loving. The next I was a crazy psycho number. I was ultra-high maintenance and Ken tried so hard to always make me happy, and when I persisted in being deliberately cold and dismissive, he'd lose his temper and see red. His eyes would spin, his hair stood up and he'd fly out of control.

Once I phoned my sister to rescue me.

"Help me, I think Ken is going to kill me," I screamed.

Ken then kicked the phone out of my hand.

My sister, who lived a 10-minute drive away, got such a fright she sped over to my house in record time. Looking through the blinds, she could see me huddled in a ball by the couch while Ken hit and kicked me. While Whitney Houston was singing her hit song "I Will Always Love You" on the radio, Ken was yelling, my sister was threatening to kick down the door and I was simply screaming blue murder.

Ken flung the door open and drove off. An hour later, I drove off with my sister. By the next day, Ken and I had made up.

Sometimes there was no reason for the attacks. A lawnmower wasn't ready and I made a calm suggestion.

"Don't get so uptight," I said. "Leave it for a week or so, the grass isn't that long."

Smack.

Once or twice, I would drive down to Natal and stay with my mum or my dad, and they would tell me to leave. My mother

IFP impis and supporters, Vosloorus (Ken Oosterbroek / PictureNET Africa)

Men at the entrance of a moving train coach reach out for a commuter (Ken Oosterbroek / PictureNET Africa)

A police security guard with a rifle in downtown Johannesburg (Ken Oosterbroek / PictureNET Africa)

Funeral, 6 April 1993 (Ken Oosterbroek / PictureNET Africa)

Gambling boys, Johannesburg, 1982 (Ken Oosterbroek / PictureNET Africa)

Golden Miles Bhudu campaigns for prisoners' rights outside the Johannesburg Supreme Court, Johannesburg, 1993. (Ken Oosterbroek / PictureNET Africa)

Kevin Carter taking pictures of photographer Ken Oosterbroek, Soweto, 1993 (Ken Oosterbroek / PictureNET Africa)

Kevin Carter (left) and João Silva at Kevin's house in the Johannesburg suburb of Troyville, 1993 (Ken Oosterbroek / PictureNET Africa)

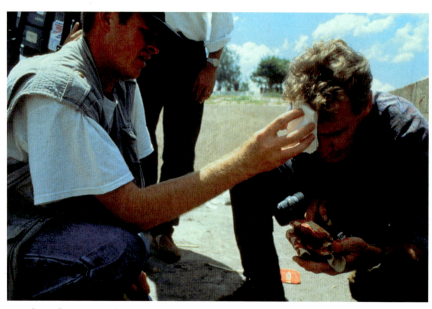

Media photographer injured by rocks thrown during riots in Bophuthatswana, 1994 (Ken Oosterbroek / PictureNET Africa)

AWB meeting, early 1990s (Ken Oosterbroek / PictureNET Africa)

Johannesburg star photographer Ken Oosterbroek, dying while covering a gun battle between ANC and IFP supporters in Tokoza township, east of Johannesburg, 18 April 1994 (João Silva/ PictureNET Africa)

ANC in Exile: Thabo Mbeki,
Lusaka, Zambia, 1985 (Steve
Hilton-Barber / PictureNET
Africa)

Swaziland National Trust
Commission Project, a sangoma,
2000 (Steve Hilton-Barber /
PictureNET Africa)

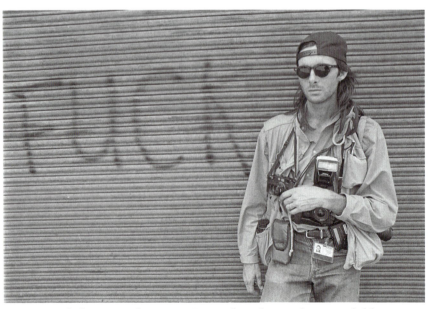

Portrait of photographer Ken Oosterbroek, no date available
(Steve Hilton-Barber / PictureNET Africa)

Sappi unhappy valley, April 2000 (Steve Hilton-Barber / PictureNET Africa)

AIDS test, date and location unknown (Steve Hilton-Barber / PictureNET Africa)

Northern Sotho initiation ceremony, Northern Province, 1990 (Steve Hilton-Barber / PictureNET Africa)

Northern Sotho initiation ceremony, Northern Province, 1990 (Steve Hilton-Barber / PictureNET Africa)

Initiates going home, Northern Province, 1990 (Steve Hilton-Barber / PictureNET Africa)

A Swazi princess and the purple crested lourie, 2000 (Steve Hilton-Barber / PictureNET Africa)

seriously did worry Ken would one day really hurt me. It sounds shocking now, especially as I sit here writing about it in Australia where everything seems so calm and ordered. According to modern first-world ideals, real men don't hit women, but in reality, many relationships have occasional violent spats. I know lots of loving relationships where the man hit the woman in the initial stages of the romance when emotions and hormones still raged silly. We were still such a young and volatile couple, so while it seems bad in today's world, in the context of our life and times, it wasn't that appalling. Ken was always deeply ashamed and horrified afterwards and never once blamed me for causing him to lash out.

I knew when I was taking arguments too far. Yet I verbally assaulted him until he cracked. Mostly, he was an overwhelmingly loving and gentle husband with only very infrequent forays to the dark side. Although Ken's upbringing is not my story to tell, he grew up in less-than-idyllic circumstances where he was exposed to drunken violence. Added to that, we lived in a country where extreme violence was integral to everything; rape was rife, and death was all around us. South Africa at the time was a bloodbath, with hundreds being slaughtered in townships weekly. Ken, and occasionally me too, worked in bizarrely bloody jobs. So being South African was dysfunctional on so many levels.

It didn't help that, work-wise, Ken was under a lot of stress and was exhausted in the last leg of the pre-election campaign. He was pulled between his ambition and his love for me.

"I can't think how to be a good husband right now. I wish I was. I wish I was a boring old fucking bank clerk or boatman.

"Mon, you know I can't be ... so let's work something out.

"I am fucked. I must, must sleep. I love you Monica with all my heart if you can only find it."

I would cope with stress by retreating to bed to sleep and read, not wanting to talk, just silent and disconnected.

And I'd wake up to notes that said:

"Be warm because I can't get through your ice ... you are my only wife, my only life ... I'm really fucked up, burnt out,

overworked and I see no end to it and I know that your life without me is impossible. I am so sorry for that. I will try ... I will try ...

"*I love you because your happiness is my happiness ...*"

And at night, we would cling to each other; our limbs wrapped together, our love the only stability in a South Africa that seemed to be spiralling out of control.

"*Moho. You know, all things said and done, I really love you deep down. I cannot make this more manifest than when I hold you in my arms and you are mine and I am yours ...*"

More strangely, Ken's violence towards me made me feel completely adored. I thrived on the attention, the passion and the drama of our fights. In some perverted way, I saw it as proof he loved me very deeply. I never, not once, fought back. I simply huddled down until his rage passed and we both looked at each other in shock, like survivors of a terrible accident. Then he would cry. I would cry. I'd feel humbled by his vulnerability and deep distress. We would make up. And be more in love than ever. And so our mad dance of love continued.

"*I'd like to tell you about strength within love; it is the strength to shape things the way you want them because you are doing it for two, not just for one. It is the strength to build and the strength to break.*

"*Ultimately, love becomes its own strength because there can be no getting away from it, it is manifest within you and is an invisible line with the one you love. It supersedes man-made boundaries and regulations, it makes easy the difficult, it is something to lean on when the ghosts plague you. It's something to get through the day with, something to live for. I am strong because I have lived love and am in love.*

"*Monica, I love you in a way which is just there; it's very strong and it's one of the reasons why I can sometimes laugh in the face of adversity because I know the reality of my existence is as solid as a rock. Life with you is the foundation of my life, my wife, and I love you forever.*"

And my heart loved him right back with an equal passion – he was mine and I was his – two unbalanced lovers wound tightly together in the maelstrom of our lives, whirling toward stable ground.

Chapter 7

I had no chance to tell Ken I loved him with all my heart. I had no time to become the kind and understanding wife I wanted to become once I sorted out my own headspace. We had no time to go into old age together to use the walking sticks given to us on our wedding day just a few years previously.

Ken had won Ilford Press Photographer of the Year four days earlier. In his Ilford catalogue for that year, he wrote:

> *To my most gorgeous wonderful wife Monica*
> *Thank you for your love – it is really all I have that is real.*
> *I love you*
> *Xxx*
> *Ken*

It was to be the last love note I received from him.

On 18 April 1994, Ken was late for work again. He was in a flap because he was late and couldn't find a black scarf he wore every day as a tribute to fellow photographer and friend Abdul Shariff, who had been shot earlier that year. I had thrown it into the laundry basket but was half asleep and too lazy to get up and find it.

"I don't know where it is," I replied.

I last saw Ken rushing out of the bedroom, without his scarf.

On the day in question, Ken went into Thokoza on the East Rand which was now the scene of politically motivated running gun battles. Hostel dwellers and the fledgling National Peace Keeping Force (NPKF) were involved in more fire fights.

Although Ken and I worked together often, that day I was working from home doing some freelance assignments. I chatted to him via phone a few times that morning (him on one of those first mobile phones, the big clunky ones the size of bricks). He'd been a little unnerved at the hectic fighting in Thokoza that day.

"It's really tense," he said. "It's not good ... police have been tuning us all day and the vibe here's really *kak*."

"Phone you later, baby."

He sounded flustered and tired. So when the phone rang again after lunch, I presumed it was him. Instead, it was American photographer Dave Brauchli, telling me Ken had been shot, caught between the NPKF and hostel dwellers.

"What? Oh my god, oh my god," I said. "What happened? Where did he get hit?"

I was hyperventilating and freaking out, trying to hear Dave above the noise of people shouting in the background. I kept firing questions, but Dave just kept telling me to call *The Star*.

I slammed down the phone and quickly dialled the news desk and got hold of the news editor's secretary.

"Shit, no, no, it's Monica, what must I do?" I heard her say.

Robin Comley, the pictures editor, came to the phone and said she would take me out to Natalspruit, the East Rand hospital Ken had been taken to. I was hysterical and couldn't explain where I lived, so, wearing bright orange shorts and a Mickey Mouse T-shirt, I leapt into my car and somehow made the 30-minute journey into town. When I got to *The Star* I saw people crying, colleagues shocked to see me, and one journalist, who saw me, said: "What are you doing HERE?" She sounded accusing and it struck me as strangely aggressive.

Peter Mogaki, a gentle colleague of Ken's, drove us to the hospital. Robin, who had been firmly instructed by *The Star*'s resident psychologist not to tell me Ken was dead, was trying to prepare me for more than the surface arm wound I somehow told myself it was. The whole way there, I plea-bargained with God, and begged Robin for reassurances that Ken was still alive.

"What would you do if he wasn't okay?" she said.

"I'd kill myself – I couldn't survive without him – it would be the end of me," I ranted on, but deep down, I believed everything was really going to be okay. Not for a moment did I seriously think he was dead.

"Make him okay, God, and I'll do 10 good deeds every day," I prayed.

I made myself promises to never argue with him again, to donate to charities and go to church every Sunday for the rest of my life.

Stepping from the car, I was confused by the barrage of local and international photographers hanging around, but they all awkwardly avoided looking at me. Some actually turned and walked quickly away when they saw me approaching them to find out Ken's whereabouts. It took a few agonising minutes before two kind colleagues fronted up and took me into a small room off the entrance.

As I walked in, I saw a body on the gurney covered with a sheet. I instantly recognised those large, worn-down sneakers and black socks hanging over the bed. I gingerly pulled the sheet down and there, looking back, was the grey, completely dead face of Ken. I asked the nurse for a cloth to wipe the dirt and blood from his face. I held his heavy, cold hand and spoke to him urgently, pleading with him to wake up.

"It's okay, my darling, I am here ... I'm here," I said.

"Open your eyes. I'll look after you ... don't worry ... I'm here now, my baby," I kept saying, over and over again.

Out of the corner of my eye, I was aware of a commotion. Some foreign photographers had crept up to televise and photograph me, and TJ Lemon, a local freelancer, had put on a large telephoto lens and was swinging it at them wildly, telling them to get out and back off.

I climbed onto the stretcher and started shaking Ken.

"Wake up, wake up," I cried.

It was then I noticed his back had already started to turn black-blue where blood had pooled. I gathered his lifeless body up against mine and started sobbing.

As they took Ken off to the morgue, I insisted he have his jacket put on and his body wrapped in a blanket because "I don't want him to be cold".

I tried repeatedly to call my father from the hospital but his line was constantly engaged. So I simply got a lift back home. Some of my family came around. Friends of Ken's before he became a photographer came round and with Ken's sister, Athelé, and her then husband, Oliver, we all sat in our lounge, stunned, trying to absorb the shock.

From eyewitness accounts following that day, it became clear that he had been caught in the crossfire between hostel dwellers and the NPKF, a skittish and poorly trained group of men put together by the interim government. According to reports on Ken's death, and from video footage taken by media at the scene, Ken was standing against a long pre-cast concrete wall between the garage forecourt and the wall of the hostel. The NPKF was lined up along the wall in among the long grass and weeds. There was a volley of shots, then Ken was filmed crumpling to the ground, a trickle of blood running out of the side of his mouth.

On news footage, João was heard screaming for soldiers to stop firing, then fellow photographer Gary Bernard and American photographer James Nachtwey lugged Ken to a nearby Buffel and loaded him in; Gary looked utterly shocked and horrified. In between shouting "Fuck, fuck" at frequent intervals, a distraught João took pictures.

Ironically, Ken was killed on the very street where he shot his memorable image of the two young girls running for their lives – the first frame he shot of the township violence in the Transvaal three years previously.

The next day, when I saw João's excellent but confronting front-page picture of a very dead Ken being carried by friends to the Buffel, a part of me was upset that João had been taking pictures of Ken. I wasn't angry with João, but I had so much anguish and confusion and nowhere to channel it. In retrospect, I know Ken would have wanted his death to be recorded and now there is comfort knowing that those pictures are part of South African history. I was then later accused of trying to prevent João from being a pall bearer at the funeral – and of not getting my own way – but in reality, I quickly calmed down when Robin Comley, as usual, stepped in with her voice of peace and reason, and I changed my mind. An unrecorded death is a forgotten death, someone once said or wrote, and I completely agree. Of course, at that time, nobody realised that Ken had been shot by a dum-dum bullet – outlawed then by the Geneva Convention – which had penetrated his chest cavity and exploded on impact, leaving no exit wound. He would have been killed immediately, so taking pictures of him made not one iota of difference as there was nothing João could have done to help Ken at that stage.

The funeral was wall-to-wall with media people, photographers, reporters, editors. Wearing a pretty floral dress Ken had bought me four months earlier as one of his many presents on my 30th birthday, I was emotionally all over the place. I giggled in the speeches, then nearly freaked out when Ken's drunk brother marched up the aisle shouting unintelligible gibberish and had to be hauled out by a security guard. Watching video footage of the funeral some years later, I was unnerved to hear primal screaming as the coffin was driven away in the hearse – and then realised it was me, crying out like a wild animal suffering. The blood-curdling wailing came from somewhere deep down inside me as I saw part of me being ripped out and driven away to be burnt to ashes.

After the funeral, my extended family and Ken's met at our house for tea and cake. Kevin popped in briefly. Robin was there. But I remember no other media people. It ended after I looked over to see Ken's father with a beer in his hand, presiding over a group of people saying: "I won't miss him much as we weren't close, but he was a fine photographer."

I'd had enough.

"Okay, everyone," I yelled. "I'm done. The party is over."

Ken's dad looked rather bemused. He said he'd leave soon, after he'd finished his drink.

"No, I want you to get the FUCK out of my house RIGHT NOW," I screamed. "GET OUT NOW!"

Everyone looked completely stunned. Once he left, some of my relatives hung around, then everyone left and it was just me and my sister, who immediately moved in to stay a while.

Most photographers kept well away from my madness. However, I do have flashes of some kind media folk listening to me waffle on and on mindlessly on the few freelance jobs I braved. The *Sunday Times* were really kind to me, particularly the news editor Jeremy Brooks, who gave me freelance work when some were afraid to even meet my eye. Well-known journalist Charmain Naidoo came over to my desk and gave me a hug, despite me previously being rude to her at a press conference when I imagined her to be flirting with Ken.

Much of my wave of support, however, came from complete strangers who wrote to me with words of comfort. Some sent mementoes; others gave me poems, music and photographs. There were hundreds of letters, vases of flowers, visitors and callers – even Winnie Mandela visited, but she had to leopard crawl in through a half-opened garage door as I had lost all the keys and remotes.

Most of all I remember the beautiful Robin Comley, who gave me all her love and support at a time her heart was broken too. An unsung hero of these dark days, Robin was always in the background, giving photographers and journalists (and me) much-needed advice, guidance and support. She held the fort together, a calm island in the storm, and a true friend to everyone. Robin compiled beautiful books for Ken's family with photographs and tributes that arrived at *The Star* following Ken's death. I am well aware of, and eternally grateful for, the way Robin protected me from so many people at a time when I was too vulnerable and mentally unstable to behave in a socially acceptable way.

In among all the beautiful messages was a touching gift – a wooden crocodile carved by a Venda artist – with a note attached.

It read: "Love is a river that runs into itself. Strength and solidarity, keeping you in my heart." It was from a photographer, Steve Hilton-Barber, who I only knew vaguely as he moved with the 'cool' people. But it wasn't long before this crocodile returned to him … circles within circles.

The days immediately after that are a blur, even though my father and family, plus Ken's sister Athelé and then husband Oliver, came to help me. The shock was so deep, real life was distant and surreal. Nothing could touch me. I felt nothing, literally nothing. I wasn't hungry, or tired; just numb. The thought of eating sickened me. I lived on coffee and started smoking. I shook all the time. I was terrified to go to sleep because waking up was too disorientating. I took handfuls of strong sleeping tablets, piled the bed heavy with blankets as Ken always slept half on top of me, but I'd sit up a few hours later, my heart thudding, wondering what was wrong. As the wave of memory flooded back, the pain swept over me until my body's natural chemicals kicked in and I was anaesthetised back to fuzzy again.

I didn't open Ken's cupboards or look in any of his drawers; I did not move anything in the house. His maroon shirt was left hanging from the curtain rail where it was the morning he left. I visually blanked out his kombi parked in the garden, and I simply imagined he was on an assignment somewhere. The moment I thought he might not be coming back, my brain would short-circuit, or I'd have a panic attack.

I felt hopeless and helpless, and completely alone. My entire world was spiralling out of control and I was unable to think clearly through the fog. I wanted to go to sleep and never wake up. The thought of living life without Ken was unbearable.

I stopped wanting visitors. So I set up a bed in my bedroom cupboards and hid there for days and days. I lived on coffee with heavy tots of marula cream liqueur, strong sleeping tablets and madness. I shook all the time and so much, I couldn't spoon my coffee into a cup without making a mess. I'd stockpile sedatives I'd collect from various doctors so I had a permanent way out if I really needed it. Just as I was about to keel over with mental and physical fatigue, my friend, recent Pulitzer Prize winner Kevin Carter, came round to visit. Still frozen beyond reach, I couldn't give him time and attention.

"I am so tired," he said.

"I can't sleep. I just keep thinking. My life is so fucked up," he said.

I gave him a packet of Rohypnol, a particularly strong sleeping tablet.

Depressed and confused, he was talking of "going to join Ken" but I thought it was just Kevin being his dramatic self.

That night, Kevin died after he parked his little red bakkie against a blue gum tree in a national reserve near his parents' home, attached a garden hose to the exhaust pipe, and rolled up the window of his car. I presume he took my sleeping tablets, and wrote until he passed out and died of carbon monoxide poisoning.

Kevin left a suicide note that read: *"I'm really, really sorry. The pain of life overrides the joy to the point that joy does not exist ... depressed ... without phone ... money for rent ... money for child support ... money for debts ... money! ... I am haunted by the vivid memories of killings & corpses & anger & pain ... of starving or wounded children, of trigger-happy madmen, often police, of killer executioners ... I have gone to join Ken if I am that lucky."*

When police phoned very early the next day to tell me Kevin was dead I actually just went back to sleep again. When friends and colleagues started calling later that day, I felt quite surprised as I'd temporarily forgotten I'd already been told.

I was not mentally well. Was it exacerbated by the fact that I already struggled with depression? Did I also suffer from Post-Traumatic Stress Disorder, considering that as a journalist I had seen so many people shot dead, kids brutalised, animals left maimed and whimpering and other such atrocities? Or was I just the narcissistic drama queen some people claimed I was? Maybe my insanity was a culmination of factors.

I felt ill when I saw couples. I talked obsessively about Ken to anyone who would listen. I told everyone I was a widow. Perhaps I thought that if I said it enough times, I could make myself believe it. Five months later, I took a trip to France to a photography exhibition showing some of Ken's work, but stopped off in Britain and got no further. Within a week of getting home, I arranged a British work permit, bought an air ticket, sold my car, the house and all its contents.

I kept only some of my clothes and special mementos of our life together: The thick file of love letters, all his diaries and poetry, a couple of books, personal photographs, our travel treasure, his shooting jacket, our collection of stuffed bears and a few of his favourite T-shirts were sorted into a large suitcase, which I still carry around wherever I go.

Packing up the house was a symbol of the end of our life together. I sobbed bitterly, not only for the loss of Ken, but for me and the end of the person I had been.

I was ready to leave South Africa. I'd experienced too much heartbreak and death and destruction. Faces of township grief haunted me. My mind was chaotic. And nowhere felt like home. In a few weeks between moving out of our home and taking off for London, I packed up Ken's kombi and took off for Cape Town where I hung out in a boarding house or lolled about on the beach, waiting for time to pass. On the way home, I managed to write off the kombi, lose my passport and have a nervous breakdown ... then ended up in hospital ... so the trip had to be postponed for a week or two.

I'd gone to the outpatients section of a clinic to get a sedative as I was really feeling hysterical and hadn't slept for days. The doctor listened to my crazy talking, then basically darted me across the room like a rhino. The next day I awoke in hospital with some fat, red-haired psychiatrist telling my family that I had bipolar disorder and insisting I went on lithium, which made me fat and sluggish overnight. He neglected to ask me if there was any reason I might have been behaving irrationally, or if I was perhaps just too tired, stressed and deeply depressed. But the moment I was out of there, I was off his psychotic drugs and flying overseas.

In Britain I discovered an utterly unfamiliar place where I felt more isolated and foreign than ever before. When Tony O'Reilly

(Heinz Beans CEO and owner of Independent Newspapers) asked me if there was anything he could do to help me, I don't think he expected me to take him up on it. But I did contact him and asked for a job on one of his newspapers in London. So initially I had work on a small Independent regional, but soon left to freelance for the Murdoch papers like *The Sun* and *The London Sunday Times*. I wasn't able to settle down or think clearly in the foreign British newspaper world, which was very competitive and challenging.

It took a year to accept that Ken was dead. When people told me there was life after death and that Ken would be waiting for me, I clung to that hope. But as the shock wore off, the pain got worse and the intense sorrow was overwhelming. Holed up in my tiny apartment in Kentish Town, I thought of all the women, many of whom I had seen and interviewed, who had lost husbands in township violence and crime. Many had coped without the emotional and financial support I had had. It made me feel weak, self-pitying and pathetic. I could not believe I would ever be happy again. Everything I did or saw, I mentally photographed onto my soul to share with Ken in the afterlife.

I worked until dark, came home to eat and watch hours of TV, then put on my long black London coat, gloves and hat and marched manically around the neighbourhood, crying and panting out plumes of frosty air until I was tired enough to sleep. One day, Alison Dow, a doctor with a practice next door to my bedsit, called over and told me to come and see her. She had been worriedly watching me. Imagine our surprise to find out that she was married to a South African, a former ANC member, and I had once written a story about her husband escaping arrest after his ANC cell was hunted down and discovered. Small world indeed! She was just one of some wonderful people who helped carry me through the first real calamity in my life.

I didn't make it easy for myself as I was lost in the sadness, too depressed to get out and meet new people and have a laugh. I was homesick. I joined a kickboxing academy across the road at the local community centre. I was the only woman and, because the area was predominantly Nigerian, I revelled in the gentlemanly attentions of these good-looking and charming sparring mates. I'd try to kick them, and they would catch my foot and then dance away, making me hop furiously forward to keep my balance. Then one day, another woman arrived, a gleaming Amazonian beauty, and they teamed us together. Within minutes, she'd kicked me in the stomach and I burst into tears. I was too scared to go back again.

Sometimes I would get lengthy phone calls from Gary Bernard who'd talk about the day Ken died and how his life was now falling apart because his work was too stressful. He committed suicide a few years later and I look back on these calls, wondering why I didn't pick up that he was so sad. As these were the days before emails, Skype and Viber, I hand-wrote letters to my family and Ken's, and waited a few weeks to get a letter in return. Robin wrote me long letters giving me all the news from *The Star*. But I heard from no one else.

Every day seemed grey and wet, with a constant gentle mist. My only comfort was the fact that from now on my life would get better. I believed that God had done his worst, I'd paid my dues, and nothing in my life would ever be this bad again.

Little did I know that this was the start of possibly the most tumultuous two decades of my life.

Chapter 8

From the moment I met Steven, I was addicted.

I arrived in Johannesburg to organise the inquest into Ken's death in April 1995, which coincided with the first anniversary of Ken's death. While it was quite understandable that Ken's family and I were still fully shocked and dazed, I was astounded at how shaken his photographic colleagues remained.

I was staying with Ken's cousin, and my close friend, Caroline Hurry, who'd arranged for us to meet up with Steven Hilton-Barber for lunch.

"Why don't you date him?" I said. "He's really sexy."

But Caroline wasn't interested.

"Nah, too many drugs … fun, but not boyfriend material," she replied.

"*Really?*" I said. "What kind of drugs?"

"Anything and everything," she replied.

The three of us met at noon in a gorgeous little Portuguese restaurant in Parktown North on the first anniversary of Ken's death, but Carrie soon left for her afternoon subbing shift at *The Saturday Star*.

One minute Steven and I were eating peri-peri chicken and drinking wine, and the next thing I was giving Steven money to buy cocaine. I was so bored with being mournful, hiding in the darkness, that I was ready to run a little wild. I'd never seen coke in my life before, but by 8pm that night, I was high as a kite on a mixture of coke and tequila. We ended up in an Auckland Park bar dancing and cavorting about, unfortunately bumping into a group of grieving journalists and photographers who'd met up to mark the anniversary of Ken's death. I was completely trashed, with Steven hanging all over me, and people were disgusted. So Steven and I drove to Hillbrow, dancing in a nightclub where only prostitutes and serious drug dealers were still awake, then went back to the share-house Steven had just moved into. All night, we talked and laughed and danced. We had just instantly clicked. It was the meeting of like minds and the connection of kindred spirits. But when I sobered up, I soon found out I was the Merry Widow personified. I'd totally lost the sympathy vote and no one in town was my friend any more. While Ken's colleagues, friends and relatives had gathered to mourn the death of Ken, I was getting fucked, literally and figuratively – and yes, I was smitten. But it came with a price: the much tut-tutting of so many forked tongues.

For the next week, Steven and I spent all my remaining time that trip very sober and quiet, simply talking and exploring, sharing ideas about how to find yourself when you get lost. We talked about our deep love for our families, fighting depression and insecurity, striving for that elusive sense of fulfilment, and discovered we shared a spontaneous and adventurous spirit. We bared our deepest vulnerabilities at a time when we were both weak and broken, but together we felt understood and strong.

Soon I returned to London. Two weeks later, Steven arrived on my doorstep and asked me to marry him. So I did.

We were wed in the Fulham Magistrate's Court in June 1995. We grabbed witnesses off the street – the Mansfield sisters, 82 and 84, who had been married to brothers and lived in the same street all their lives although they went to Brighton on their honeymoon. The carved wooden crocodile given to me the previous year by Steven when we hardly knew each other came along as our private witness. I wore a short leather dress with braids in my hair, and Steven had on black chinos and a brightly coloured

T-shirt. We danced to M People's "Open Up Your Heart", took official wedding pictures in a phone booth at the train station, and enjoyed a celebratory lunch at a crazy Greek restaurant in Covent Gardens. The carved crocodile was now back in Steven's life.

Filled with the euphoria of the newly betrothed, we excitedly told the waiter we had just got married.

"Don't worry," he said sourly. "You can always get divorced."

We bought a cheap camper van and headed out of London for wonderful adventures in Cornwall, Wales and Ireland, and even got to Malaga and Barcelona in Spain.

Ironically, we spent the money made by Ken during the elections, money Ken and I had planned to use after the elections for a long trip overseas to chill out and get our perspective back on life. And yes, I did feel incredibly sad and guilty – and part of me resented Steven for being with me spending Ken's money – but it seemed churlish to be the killjoy and I longed to just break free after the years of hard work and depression.

So we ate and drank merrily, went clubbing where I took ecstasy for the first time, discovered I adored happy house music and fell madly in love. Steven, fairly recently out of rehab, got fit, brown and healthy as we jogged on Hampstead Heath, explored every quaint town, village and city by foot, and adventured energetically morning to night.

We were swamped by angels during a fancy-dress parade in Bath, chased by a bull in a field outside Cornwall, thoroughly soaked in torrential rain on the Isle of Skye while hiking, played endless games of pool and darts from pub to pub, ate strawberries and cream in Wimbledon during Wimbledon, and swam through the Lake District. Life was a blur of galleries, symphonies, churches, rock concerts and museums; our brains filled with creative overload. We enjoyed picnics in parks, boating on the River Thames, day-tripping to Blackpool and Brighton, climbing Mt Nevis, hunting down the Loch Ness monster and exploring gardens all over Britain.

One evening, partying in Wales, we were caught up in a pub argument about who should be darts secretary for the year. When the locals started drawing us into an increasingly bitter debate, Steven and I ran for it ... and impulsively caught the ferry from Fishguard to Dublin. For six weeks, we travelled round the island in our camper van, hung upside down on the cliffs of Mohair, joined in sing-alongs in Limerick, spent R1 000 on a bottle of Moët in The Temple Bar in Dublin, and heard via a sobbing fan in a bar in Derry, that Superman, Christopher Reeves, had fallen off a horse and was paralysed. Then we were robbed. Our camper van was broken into and many of our possessions, including a guitar Ken had bought me, were stolen. I lay in the street and sobbed so hard, the attending police referred us to a tourism service aiding crime victims. This organisation allowed us to phone home to cancel credit cards and order more. Moreover, they put us up for two nights in a hotel, with meals included.

But we were too tired to enjoy the luxury. It had been raining non-stop for six weeks, which was starting to get bloody depressing. Steven wobbled.

"I am fucking sick of you carrying on and on about Ken," he yelled. "Who cares about a fucking guitar? I'll get you another one."

We lost our way to the hotel. As we screamed at each other, he kept lifting his hand, threatening to hit me. I cringed. He shouted and waved his hands around more while I sat quietly trying to blend into the car seats.

It took the shine off Ireland. So we decided to put it behind us and fly to Spain where our chances of summer sunshine and warmth were excellent.

And it was glorious.

We were nearly run over by a herd of goats in Malaga, ate paella and drank carafes of red wine on the Costa del Sol and swam in the greasy Mediterranean. We hung out in Barcelona where we sun-baked on the Barcelona beach, danced up and down La Rambla, the wide boulevard stretching from Plaça de Catalunya to Port Vell, then wandered around the Gothic district (Barri Gòtic), El Raval and El Born. We had no money to go clubbing but we enjoyed the music and vibe pumping into the streets until early every morning. We'd drink cheap wine and dance on the pavement in the late-night sunshine.

Postcards were only sometimes sent correctly. Writing postcards together in a tiny Andalusian village, Steven was enjoying his morning cigar with a short black coffee and cognac. So I grabbed the cards and took them off across the road and posted them in what I thought was a post box. It turned out to be a bank receptacle for cheque deposits. While Steven fell off his chair laughing at me, I used interpretive dance to ask the village bank clerk to open the box and return my postcards.

The 1995 Rugby World Cup, when Francois Pienaar and his team had a stunning last-minute victory, was part of our travel experience. When we were in the UK and Cornwall, we watched the first round of games in pubs along with locals and tourists, many of whom were Australian and South African. For the final on 24 June, however, we were in Barcelona staying in a room with no television. To find a venue showing the game proved hopeless. Sports bars refused to turn to the rugby because soccer was on, one café owner wouldn't change channels because he was watching a popular Spanish quiz show, and we eventually took a taxi to a large international hotel, begging them to put us in touch with any South Africans staying there who we were sure would let us watch with them. If we'd had money, we would have rented a room. But we were too poor and the staff just laughed at us. In the end, we read the result – a one-liner in a Spanish paper the following day. We felt a pang of profound homesickness at that moment and always regretted missing watching this historic game live on TV.

Dad and Gail stayed a short time in my London bedsit and had packed it all up and sent it back to South Africa for me. So when Steven and I returned to London, we went via Dublin to pick up our van, then to Belsize Park where we rented a tiny bedsit. It was a gloriously hot summer and we knew we'd soon have to stop holidaying and start working as our money had all been spent. So we threw ourselves into enjoying the last of our honeymoon by indulging in every interesting and free thing possible in London. Often, we'd splash out on a West End show, buying the cheapest tickets at the least popular times. When the curtains opened, we'd skedaddle to the empty seats near the front. Such was Steven's boyish charm, no usher ever complained and, in fact, many helped us secure the best possible seats in the house.

After being cold and dried up and miserable for so long, Marriage Two was like getting into a hot bath – utter bliss – and I absolutely loved this incredibly loving and woolly man, and life continued its manic roller-coaster ride with the two of us flying from one mad adventure to another. Straight from my first love to my soul mate … in just one year! Who would have thought that Steven, a recovering crack and smack addict, plus me – the uptight teetotalling crazy woman – would make such a profound connection?

We gave each other a renewed sense of hope and excitement, reignited our passion for life, and the possibilities together seemed endless. Between us we became the Hill-Billy Barbers – and our eight years of marriage were the trip of a lifetime. Perhaps, in hindsight, if I'd known how turbulent my years with Steve would be, I might have run. But I fell in love with him and nothing – no warnings, no advice and no flash of common sense – would have stopped me from being with him.

Chapter 9

Our return to Johannesburg in late 1995 was met with a frosty reception from former friends and colleagues. Neither of us was forgiven for falling in love too soon for protocol. This was clear when we celebrated our marriage with a lunch-time ceremony at the Johannesburg Country Club for our old friends and former colleagues.

It was a simple but stylish wedding overlooking the lush country club lawns and we'd organised beautiful flowers, this time a long and flowing wedding gown and three-piece suit, harpist in the corner, and surrounded by friends and family. Some guests embraced us, but others were stony-faced, only there to satisfy some perverted curiosity, and one person even walked out, which upset me for years afterwards.

Ken's family, though invited, declined to attend, which I completely understood and respected, but I had wanted to invite them considering the love and support they had shown me following Ken's death. I still consider the whole large and strange Oosterbroek clan my family today.

Meeting Steven's charismatic family was more intimidating, mainly because they are utterly charming, incredibly smart and creatively offbeat with very proper British colonial undertones. We had a second wedding celebration up at their family's ancestral farmstead, Kings Walden Lodge in Agatha outside Tzaneen. Steven's brother Brett and sister Bridget are both dynamic over-achievers – scary if you only know them by reputation – and I was more than a little daunted by their glamorous mother, Tana. While they were all unfailingly polite, welcoming and warm, I was nervously awkward, which I covered up with unrestrained displays of obnoxious bluster that only Steven understood.

On my first visit to their fruit and nut farm outside Tzaneen, I stood with Steven and his parents with our sundowners, looking out over their valley of mango, avocado and pecan trees.

"So, which are my trees now," I joked brightly. "Can I name them?"

The family looked at me, startled.

ARGHHH!

I was also terrified that Steven would relapse into drugs on our return to Johannesburg. I stuck to him like glue, which wasn't hard since we shared a car and were together 24/7. But on the odd occasion he would venture out without me, I would look at him very carefully on his return. I hated him mixing with anyone linked to his druggie past and certainly kept him well away from anyone I considered dodgy. I secretly searched his pockets for signs of Rizlas or dope, and constantly nagged him about giving up smoking and alcohol.

My insecurity and jealousy annoyed him but he too had issues. I took him to the cemetery at St Martins-in-the-Veld where Ken was buried, and he pee'd on Ken's memorial bench. I wasn't allowed to hang Ken's pictures in our home and was never encouraged to talk about my life with Ken. That was, for him, a closed chapter in my life. Once he introduced me as "my second-hand wife". I laughed because I found it funny. Plus, I would have been worried if he didn't care enough to be jealous.

What wasn't easy was that we arrived back from London shortly before the inquest into the death of Ken. Day after day, I sat in the courtroom and watched television footage of Ken dying. Sitting through the inquest, I saw Ken die from every angle, witnessed the volley of bullets, heard the grunt of pain, and Ken clutching his chest and falling forward. I saw news clips of photographers shouting for the National Peace Keeping Force to cease fire, and hysterical colleagues lifting his lifeless body onto the back of the Buffel. I watched in horror as, again and again, I saw his familiar head flopped back, a thin trickle of blood running from the corner of his mouth to his ear.

We heard how there had been an entry wound but no exit wound – his chest blown out completely.

I had no idea of the damage done by the bullet until I went to the inquest.

The bullets are themselves grotesque, let alone the outcome they promise. They are modelled on a design called "Black Talon", said to be famous, and so named because once they impact the body, the bullets expand into jagged 'talons' that tear through flesh and maximise organ damage. Such expanding bullets, also called hollow-point bullets or 'dum-dums', are considered so cruel they were banned from use in international warfare under the Hague Convention of 1899.

This was the government's bullet of choice for the untrained and skittish National Peace Keeping Force; this is what they were given to keep peace among conflicting factions before the 1994 elections.

"If the bullet had gone in at a different angle, could he have survived?" I asked an official holding the autopsy result.

With that, the man whipped open his briefcase and pulled out blown-up pictures of Ken taken on the slab at the morgue, with his chest split down the middle with skin, ribs and flesh peeled back. The man showed me how his chest cavity had been completely blown out.

"Here, you can take these copies," he insisted. "You can put them in your photo album."

Media at the inquest came over to see the pictures, but as Ken was naked and the pictures showed him full-length, I got Robin Comley to intervene and make him put the pictures quickly away.

For much of the court case I vacillated between snickering and snorting derisively at evidence from the aggressive Defence Force, and giggling at evidence from João, who described events of the day with such strong language and wild gesticulations the entire court, including the judge, battled to keep a straight face.

At one point, when I dropped a pencil, Steven and a member of the NPKF bent down to pick it up and clashed heads under the bench.

"I didn't know whether to swear at him, or thank him," Steven quipped.

We had a small-time lawyer from my home town of Pieter-maritzburg chosen by me before *The Star* offered to cover the legal costs – but we were up against the best the government could muster, so we were hopelessly outclassed.

Despite overwhelming evidence and ballistics proving that only the peacekeepers were close enough to have shot and killed him, the magistrate ruled that no one could be found responsible for Ken's death. However, fellow photographer Greg Marinovich told me he had been contacted by one of the peacekeepers who had been fighting in Thokoza the day of Ken's death. Greg said that the man had admitted that, out of fear and panic, the peacekeepers had unthinkingly opened fire.

Greg quotes the former NPKF officer as as saying: "I think, somewhere, somehow ... I think somewhere, one of us, the bullet that killed your brother – it came from us."

Ken's colleagues and family put so much energy and time into the inquest, sticking it out despite knowing it would be hard to prove the NPKF responsible, and photographers openly wept when the case ended unsatisfactorily.

Ken's colleagues and family bonded during the weeks in court while I, by remarrying, had become the outsider. Everyone seemed to dive in and claim parts of Ken for themselves, and people who were once an integral part of my life had now become strangers. With Steven aggressively pulling me into a new life, and me wanting to cling to the old, I was being torn apart.

In some ways, the end of the inquest was sad, as it had been something of Ken to cling to, and a reason to talk about him, so all I was left with now were my memories, more than a dash of bitterness and my suitcase of memorabilia stashed in a cupboard.

But for a lot of it, I was cushioned and protected by my great bear of a husband – who took over my life and corrupted my lifestyle in both good ways and bad.

Chapter 10

Travelling for me is a mystical experience. It's a complete adrenalin blast where senses are filled to overflowing, the brain is active and you feel truly alive. Travel stimulates dopamine and endorphins – a bit of a rush, really – and it's pretty addictive. Steven was the first person I ever met who liked to travel as much and as impulsively as I did.

One of the first places we headed off to was Venda in the very north of South Africa, a mythical paradise of diverse beauty and antiquity ripe for exploring. The attraction for Steven was the host of talented artists living in the area, in particular the charismatic prophet, Jackson Hlungwani, carver of the wooden crocodile Steven sent me after Ken died.

Perched on a well-wooded hill overlooking a small village, we found Hlungwani sitting next to a fire, carving a lion from a gnarled piece of marula wood while listening to a Venda music programme on a radio that was hanging precariously from an old fig tree.

Head Priest of his African Independent One-Time Church, at the time Hlungwani had lived in his home for 40 years – and it was guarded by a large dead crocodile that had been preserved with its mouth propped open by a German beer bottle. He took time out from his carving to bless Steven's new possessions – me, and our recently purchased car, a Toyota Corolla.

With the Soutpansberg mountains, clear lakes and some of the finest indigenous forests in southern Africa – with black ivory, yellowwood, kiaat, stinkwood and fig trees – it's easy to see why so many of the Venda are inspired to become artists. Together, in our new second-hand car, we passed through remote villages with panoramic landscapes steeped in folklore, stopping to look at the sacred and spiritual Lake Fundudzi and the Thathe Vondo Forest with its giant hardwood, waterfalls, canopies of tree ferns and creepers.

We visited another highly entertaining carver, Albert Munyai, a hyperactive and inspired artist who regaled us with visions of truths told through work, where he explained how the wood spoke to him. Further down the track, Johannes Maswanganyi greeted us warmly while his children ran up dispensing hugs and kisses, chickens jumped in our car and goats and dogs crowded around to sniff our bottoms.

"I'd hate to move from here to a jingly place where there's no time to think," Johannes told me. I totally understood that.

All around Venda, Steven was enthusiastically received by old acquaintances, and his amiable and affectionate charm won him new friends everywhere. This was so typical of Steven, sincerely connecting with all sorts of people wherever he went, taking me to places I'd never been before, and opening me up to the magical African culture. As we travelled, we relished the mental and physical liberation of road-tripping.

Hot on the heels of that Venda trip, in February 1996, we took off on a travel-magazine commission to Uganda, where we were privileged to be part of a luxury safari to track gorillas, learn more about chimpanzees, and meet the warm and generous people in that beautiful country.

One fine day, we headed off on a borrowed bone-shaking 125cc motorbike for 56 kilometres from Fort Portal to the Semliki Valley to visit the Ntandi pygmy tribe, against the advice of the tourism department.

Bouncing down the steep pass, we passed thickly forested ravines, waterfalls and lush green valley floor stretching as far as the eye could see. Swarms of butterflies flittered about and blue-headed lizards, basking in the warm sun, streaked up rock faces as we passed. As we approached the village we were stopped by a pygmy delegation brandishing pangas.

"*Mzungus, Mzungus*," they cried.

There was no turning back. By blocking the road behind us, they forced us forward toward the village, with others jogging next to us, making our escape impossible.

A rather lanky pygmy with very squint eyes pushed through the crowd that had gathered around us as we got off our bike. After haggling, we paid him a $25 cover charge. This got us a vague dance, with a few unenthusiastic women with tits on the ground stomping around in a circle a few times while bashing lethargically on a broken plastic container. The sullen menfolk lurked in the background, eyeing us suspiciously while they drank beer and smoked. As we made to leave, the men came forward to aggressively sell us a bunch of poorly made bracelets.

More professional was our highly organised trip into the Bwindi Impenetrable Forest to track the endangered mountain gorillas. The guide first checked us out for colds and gave us tips on how to behave when we came across these rare creatures.

"If you are sick, the gorillas will catch your cold and die," he said.

Then he looked over at me wearing shorts and long socks.

"Missus," he said, "put on long pants."

But no, I knew better … I knew the socks would protect my legs.

Armed with sturdy walking sticks and nervous tummies, we hacked our way through the dense undergrowth. Tripping and tumbling, slipping and sliding in the steeply forested landscape, progress was slow. Often we walked in darkness as vegetation completely blocked out the light. Monkeys and chimpanzees chattered warnings, insects buzzed and the multitudinous birdsong added to the forest symphony.

"Fuck, it's a bit too bloody outdoorsy for me," I complained.

Then we walked into a clearing, and there they were – a silver-back male gorilla, a female and her baby. Steven clicked away. A few minutes later, the heavens opened and we stood in the downpour, gazing at the glossy, pitch-black gorillas eating plants only metres away. The animals tolerated our presence, while they methodically pulled off plant stems, daintily peeled off the outside layering and nibbled the soft inner flesh. Raindrops glistened on their fur and rolled off when they leant forward to eat. As water ran into the silverback's eyes, he grunted with annoyance and swabbed his forehead like a sportsman wiping sweat from his brow.

The next morning, I awoke with massively swollen legs so itchy I wanted to rip them off. I had been attacked by poisonous ivy and grasses, as the guide had politely tried to warn me.

Off to the hospital I went.

Under 'Tribe', the nurse wrote: "*Mzungu.*"

The nurses all came out to look at my swollen, spotty legs and there was much consternation and sympathy, but the young Polish doctor merely gave me a few antihistamine pills and told me not to scratch.

"You probably need an antihistamine injection, but we have nothing like that out here so you'll just have to tough it out," she said.

Steven decided to buy litres of waragi gin, a local alcoholic beverage similar to *witblitz* or a crude form of vodka, and every time I felt pain, I glugged straight from the bottle. Three days later, except for the unsightly skin blotches, I was back on the road again.

Another memorable excursion was trekking through the Kibale National Forest hunting down wild chimpanzees, then heading over to Ngamba Island Chimpanzee Sanctuary on Lake Victoria to see the work being done to rehabilitate captured or injured chimps. But it was the adorable chimps at the Entebbe Wildlife Centre that captured my heart and gave me fleas.

The chimps were just like cute children. Most of them victims of the illegal chimp trade, these creatures hugged and kissed, cuddled and put their hands in ours, pulling Steven and me along to show us their cages.

"Help, help," I heard Steven cry.

I turned around to see one mischievous chimp with his long arms up Steven's shorts holding onto his dangly bits.

"Don't just stand there laughing – do something," he yelled.

Before I had a chance to step forward, another chimp quickly snatched a lens from Steven's camera bag while a third leapt off the fencing onto Steven's head where he proceeded to tug his hair.

I wanted to help but it was so funny, I was doubled over guffawing so hard I nearly wet my pants.

A few months later, Steven and I headed off on another big adventure. We planned to travel 2 000 kilometres on a raft down the flooded Limpopo River through Botswana, Zimbabwe, South Africa and Mozambique. We wanted to explore the river described by Rudyard Kipling in the *Just So Stories* as "the great, grey-green greasy Limpopo all set about with fever trees". For millennia, the Limpopo has carved its way through the land and beckoned communities to its shores. Even when dry on the surface, it remains one of Africa's largest underground rivers, supplying millions of people in Africa with water. It's hard to imagine that water welling up from the earth in the centre of Johannesburg trickles through concrete canals before branching into the Jukskei River, which flows into the Crocodile River, which converges with the Marico River at Roodepoort to become the mysterious Limpopo River, tearing through volcanic rock and tumbling down valleys into the Indian Ocean.

Hopelessly under-prepared and poorly equipped, we went where no man had gone before – mainly because of the Mozambican war and the unrest in Zimbabwe, and the fact that for most of the time, unless in flood, much of the river is shallow or underground. Now it was a raging river, as wide as 17 kilometres in many places.

With just a 40-horsepower Mariner engine and two stoners in a 4x4 as back-up crew, we puttered along, learning to read the river, occasionally coming across a settlement where the locals were fascinated to see white faces. Our land crew, two unemployed stoners from Nelspruit, were never at the appointed place as arranged and often we were very, very lost, as the roads were few and impossible to navigate with the floods.

Too often we raced towards waterfalls and weirs, and only by the god of good luck did we actually not kill ourselves.

"Turn the boat round," I screamed out on our second day on the river. "Else we're going over."

But it was too late. Clinging to safety ropes, we steeled ourselves as we were swept down into the water below. The next second, the boat bounced down and water flew over our heads, spitting us out of the whirlpool into the calm current beyond, and off we pottered again, hearts pounding.

Crocodiles lurked, and we nearly bumped into a hippo on several occasions.

"Check out that grey rock just ahead of us," I said on day three. Next thing, the 'rock' opened its huge mouth and I was looking down an enormous pink tunnel.

Most of the time, we couldn't find our crewmen – the road and the river seldom met, especially because of the floods – so it was a bit hit and miss. When we did, we got stuck constantly and had to dig the 4x4 out of puddles so big, mud crept in through the windows. And when we came across a stream too deep to cross, we would have to turn around and fight our way back through the bush to find another route.

On the river, we passed neat villages of wooden huts with verandas and elevated storage bins, clichéd African postcard scenes blurring and disintegrating: mealie fields and vegetable patches ploughed by oxen, goats and cattle herded by young boys and penned up at night, chickens in thatched coops, women under trees milling maize in wooden pots while men huddled together in discussion, gracefully swaying girls carrying brightly coloured plastic water containers on their heads, and endless families in the water washing clothes and lying them out on nearby rocks to dry.

Of course, because of the war, the river banks and surrounds were areas with many undiscovered landmines, so everywhere we walked we had to take extreme care. It didn't help that I was attacked by Lariam psychosis, where the anti-malaria drugs caused crazy dreams and slight paranoia and panic. I became claustrophobic with all the overgrowth and trees closing in on me from all sides, plus the idea that there was no quick way out. One day, instead of enjoying the glorious sensation of being out in the wild on a crazy adventure, I was actually praying for immediate escape.

"Please God, let us hit a landmine so I can get away from the trees," I said one night.

"Close your eyes and sleep," Steven said. "Then the trees will go away."

"But they will be there in the morning, waiting for me again," I cried.

So Steven made me a couple of cups of hot chocolate laced heavily with sambuca, which helped. It was the last time I ever took Lariam, deciding to take my chances with malaria. Soon after I learnt that it was better not to take Lariam in malaria-ridden countries because it masks the symptoms of cerebral malaria, which could cause fatal delays in treatment.

On the final evening of our trip, racing along the river towards Xai-Xai before nightfall, light turned soft and orange-pink, filtering through the thick, enigmatic mangrove forests. It was just Steven and me, the deep droning of the boat and water splashing.

Between our travels, we bought a flat in Killarney, frighteningly close to the temptations of the seedy drug haven of Hillbrow. When we were out adventuring, everything between us was idyllic. But when we stayed home, trouble began to brew.

Chapter 11

Drugs were always the spectre looming in the background. To stop Steven going out and bingeing on narcotics, thereby emotionally and physically abandoning me, we started occasionally doing cocaine together, about once a month, wasting thousands of rands on stuffy noses, thick heads and bleeding sinuses. It was a time of manic highs and lows, hanging around dives near Ponte, the massive high-rise and Johannesburg drug mecca, waiting for dealers, then throwing away notebooks with their numbers the following day, promising NEVER AGAIN – until the next time.

It was the fastest way to feel good quickly. The thought of scoring, then cutting the coke and making it into neat little lines – and the heady rush that hits after a giant snort – was thrilling. In that coked-up time, we talked a lot about the intimacies of our lives, baring our souls and thereby becoming incredibly close while we sorted through many, many issues. It was really exciting and fun. Until the next day, when life became so grey and bleak, and we had to start putting our lives back together all over again. And so, for weeks, we'd be super-fit and healthy, full of plans and ideas, managing to do heaps of interesting freelance work. And then, we'd have the idea:

"Hey, let's treat ourselves to a bit of coke – just a gram or two."

And we'd binge for a night – then swear ourselves off it again – forever – again.

But, sadly, it wasn't long before drugs were no longer 'recreational' for Steven and he seriously relapsed – and I caught him out smoking crack and smack behind my back. The first time I knew he was smoking crack, he came back after a rare outing without me and I confronted him in the corridor of our Killarney apartment.

"What the fuck have you been doing?" I screamed. He just stared at me, his dilated eyes twirling in his head, beads of sweat above his lip, skin white and clammy.

He tried to tell me a bunch of nonsense – none of which made sense – and I went hysterical with pain and fright and terror – biting, kicking, screaming, sobbing.

"How could you do this to me?" I kept yelling. "What am I supposed to do now?"

The second time, I caught him in a spare room, smoking heroin. I'd woken up and found the bed empty and went looking for him.

"Come on, babe, can't you just relax about it and we can cuddle up together," he tried to calm me down.

We were about to head off on a trip to the USA and had booked our tickets. Clearly he must have been seriously out of his mind if he thought I was going to be okay with crack and heroin. I went crazy. There was much throwing of stuff and screaming, a few slaps and punches thrown on both sides. By 9am, I had kicked him out, cancelled our flights and packed his remaining stuff in the downstairs garage. I was so hurt, so angry, and so embarrassed to admit my marriage was already over before a year was out.

A few days later, we spoke on the phone and he said how very sorry he was, how he deeply loved me and couldn't live without me – and because I was seriously love-sick, we got back together again and rebooked out flights.

"Do you promise me you will never, ever touch any drug again?" I pleaded.

"I can't promise, I can only try," he replied.

But I kept saying: "You have to promise, else I can't do this – promise me, please, promise me."

Yet part of me was also saying: "Don't go back, Monica. This is not a life for you. This is not love, it's compulsive behaviour, naked and humiliating neediness. This is lunacy."

But my heart won when Steven finally did promise – but deep down, I knew I'd forced him to say something he didn't really believe he could honour.

We first flew in to London, where I sat with a friend of mine for coffee while Steven went off on his own – our relationship was feeling bruised and fragile. Ali, the doctor I'd met in London after Ken's death, was very frank.

"In my work, I deal with addicts all the time," she said. "And the prognosis is not good for recovery … An addict remains an addict and, no matter what, continues to have life-long addictions."

At best, she said, the addictions could be contained to food, coffee and cigarettes, but mostly addicts fought an ongoing battle for sobriety with relapse after relapse.

I just prayed for a miracle – in my heart I told myself that if he loved me enough, and found true fulfilment through work, he wouldn't want to keep self-destructing and relapsing. The fact that I never saw the druggie side of him at all for the first six months of our marriage, where he was perfectly sober and really happy, made me cling to hope like a limpet.

We spent time in New York where we stayed in a very low-budget hotel in the city centre – and I was trapped between the bathroom and the bed by an enormous rat. I ran downstairs, Steven following behind, to beg the front desk receptionist to get someone to help us get rid of it.

The enormous turban-wearing man at the desk looked bewildered by my panic, then looked over my head to speak to Steven.

"In the Indian army we used to catch rats with our hands and eat them," the man said.

He laughed heartily, then sent someone up with a few traps, which he put under the bed, along with the half-dozen other traps

I then also saw when he lifted up the night frill.

Despite our dramatic first night, we had a gloriously exciting week, sightseeing and visiting all the galleries. We'd start the day with a glazed doughnut (or more for Steven) and cup of sweet, strong coffee for our dawn walk in Central Park. We'd then walk the city flat until late, late at night.

Some days we'd jump on the subway and catch a train for an hour to Coney Island to see this run-down former entertainment hub. Now it's been renovated and the area has become an amusement park, but then it was delightfully neglected with a couple of circus sideshows and freaky people, including dwarves and midgets, some dancing mice, a flea circus and one very, very hairy lady with an impressive beard and moustache. We kissed on top of the Empire State Building, strolled bravely through downtown Brooklyn, admired the Statue of Liberty on a tour in a boat off the Island of Manhattan, and took photos to look like we were holding the Twin Towers in our hands.

For two weeks, we spent time in Washington babysitting a friend's cats and home while she and her husband were away on their summer holidays. It was a time of festivals, music and dance, July 4th celebrations, and weather so hot, we could no longer walk hand in hand, but simply held each other's pinkies. One day, we wandered from the white area to the dark side where, watching a crack deal go down, a massive rat ran over my foot. We gave up coffee for a week, then went to Starbucks in DuPont Circle and had two massive triple-shot coffees and felt like we were going to take off. Every morning, we'd jog, very slowly, through Washington Zoo and I'd stop to admire the bears, wondering which one went best with my hair colour. For tourists with a limited budget, Washington was phenomenal – Capitol Hill, the Washington Monument, the Smithsonian and endless visits to Georgetown markets.

Then we flew into San Francisco where we met up with Mike Persson (from the Bang Bang Club days) and his new wife, and we stayed on her parents' luxurious yacht in Oakland, home of Berkeley university and drive-by shootings. Three weeks on, we hired a car and went off to Las Vegas where we took a wrong turn and ended up on the dark side – where druggies and local misfits hung out. There we bumped into a couple – a fallen football hero and his girlfriend who also happened to be the mother of his wife – an actual mother-fucker! Together we took speed and drank tequila – until we went back to their place and discovered they were into smoking speed – now known as ice – so while Steven and I were really trashed, we were also shocked enough to stagger back to our hotel. Two days later, we left Vegas with the ringing of slot machines in our ears and lights flashing in our eyes, driving across Death Valley, possibly the most silent place in the world. The hottest and driest spot in North America, the rainfall averages 5 centimetres annually and most of the desert is 282 feet (86 metres) below sea level. Harshly desolate and spectacularly white, the juxtaposition between Vegas and desert was so enormous, the trip was an out-of-body experience.

We went back through the State of California, with the blonde swaying grass and gentle blue skies, and an idyllic seaside village called Cape Town, where the population was only five, and a grizzly bear had recently broken into a house and trashed the place. We were shown the bear's footprints and teeth marks.

Seattle was a city we had enormous fun discovering, walking and driving from one side to the other, finding a host of quirky people and interesting scenarios. One day, after being amused by the staff at the famous fish markets, a man wandered over to talk to us wearing a full Bugs Bunny suit. He was even eating a carrot. When I asked if he was going to a kids' party or was a character in some performance somewhere, he merely said: "No, I just woke up this morning and felt like being a bunny." The strange man-child offered to let me wear his nose and ears for a while, which I did. Steven shared his carrot.

One of the many things Steven and I shared was a great love of early mornings, and we used to walk many, many mornings during our marriage, together watching cities come to life. Hand in hand, we would just head off, end up in a coffee shop somewhere, and then meander our way back – ranging from Johannesburg and Cape

Town to London, Dublin, New York, Cairo, Kampala, Maputo and more. But Seattle was particularly interesting. We stumbled across an amazing diner, which hosted a startling breakfast club. From what we could gather from eavesdropping on their conversations, most of the group were alcoholic men who seemed to go between living rough or in shelters. As each man trouped in, the waitress would pour him a vodka and orange juice and give it to him with a straw. Each man had such shaking hands they wobbled their way through the first drink and she had the second waiting. She even lit a cigarette and handed it over. This ritual was repeated as each man, freshly showered and cleanly dressed, staggered in. They would regale each other with wild stories of their night – and fill each other in on the many blank spots – and there would be a lot of laughing and teasing. We returned on several mornings, and each time, it was the same ritual. It was quite extraordinary.

Steven and I danced at the foot of the theatrical Badlands Wall in South Dakota, beneath the sharply eroded buttes, pinnacles and spires, before cruising through the prairies, visiting rodeos and attending greyhound races. The dramatic geological spectacles just blew us both into another stratosphere, from the awe-inspiring grandeur of Yosemite to the Blue Ridge Mountains and the Rockies. One week we were rafting down the Colorado River in summertime while singing John Denver songs, and the next we were at Old Faithful in Yellowstone National Park, watching this ancient hot spring steam, bubble and erupt.

I learnt to appreciate the free hand in bars. Tip well once and the drinks are poured without a tot measure. And in small towns, so many friendly folk buy drinks, there is soon a long line of drinks waiting. Any drinks I couldn't manage – two was usually my absolute limit – Steven was right there to help me finish up. On one of these nights, we bumped into a couple in a delightful little place called Kettle Falls – a banker who met his wife, a cleaner, in the bank toilets. They took us by boat up a river to a place called Daisy for what they promised us was the best burger in the country. The burgers were certainly pretty big and juicy!

While it was an amazing trip in a country that blew my mind

away with its incredible beauty and diversity, towards the end of the trip, there was an underlying friction, especially when I started facing the future back home. Worry turned me into a nagging, neurotic cow and Steven felt trapped, so was aggressive and sullen. I still felt shattered and insecure about his relapse, and was the constant policewoman. So Steven drank a lot of vodka and at times became quite bad-tempered and snappy.

The tension came to a head in New Orleans where he and I had an enormous fight. I was flirting with a member of a jazz band playing in some touristy bar and Steven, who was hugely drunk, stood up, dumped his drink on my head and stormed off. I ran after him.

"Come back," I yelled. "I don't know where we're staying."

But he ignored my shouting, jumped in the car and weaved off, leaving me standing in the middle of Bourbon Street. The motel receipt was in the hired car but, fortunately, I had the purse and therefore the money. I started walking off in the direction I imagined we had come from, and half an hour or so later Steven drove past, a complete coincidence. It was pure luck we found each other again. But it was not a happy reunion. Steven wanted to pack and leave to carry on the trip without me cramping his style. He punched a hole in the windscreen of the car, I clung to his legs and hung on while he tried to beat me off.

"Fuck off," he screamed. "Leave me alone – just give me some money to stay a bit longer, and you go home."

"NOOOOOO, don't leave me," I screamed.

By now the irate motel manageress was instructing us to shut up or leave, because we were screaming and crying in the car park. In the end, I forced Steven to take a sleeping tablet or two. But we were both stressed and sad the next day ... Steven sullen and aggressive, me whingeing and haranguing.

There was also another humiliating incident later in San Francisco near the end of the three-month trip. Steven was angry because I was giving him a hard time about his drinking. We were saying goodbye to Steven's San Francisco friends and continuing to argue with each other. Suddenly, Steven spat in my face and pushed me into flower beds. Nobody had ever spat in my face – and has never done so since – and it made me feel more debased and humiliated then if he'd slapped me across the face.

We returned to Johannesburg. I clung, terrified to get a job and have a life outside Steven in case he relapsed. After spending almost the whole first year of our marriage travelling and having the most incredible adventures, it was time to settle down. But neither of us knew how to do that together. We fought about money because I was 'stingy' and he was a spendthrift. I shopped at Checkers and he wanted Woolworths food only. He loved to eat out but I hated wasting money on restaurants.

So he relapsed ... again. Did our marriage fuel his relapse or did his addiction destroy our marriage? We married in haste and everyone said it wouldn't last. We were both broken people when we met, so it stood to reason we would have found it hard to pull through. He'd stood by me during the inquest and put up with living in Ken's shadow, and of constantly being compared to Ken by all my friends and family, including me, during our marriage thus far. But I'd had enough. So once again I kicked him out, and by now I was really fed up and ready to move on in my life.

Steven disappeared. I packed up our apartment, rented it out and went back to America, this time to Los Angeles to work with American actor, writer and director Emilio Estevez on a movie project he wanted to do on Ken and Kevin. It had been in the pipeline for some time, but obviously Steven didn't want me to be involved. With Steven now not a factor, the timing was perfect. I made arrangements and left.

I was met at the airport by a man carrying a board with my name – and was whisked off in a cool limousine to a fancy hotel in the trendy part of Los Angeles. The next day, I went to the Hollywood studios – driving around in a little golf buggy – and hung out with Emilio and his friends for a few days. It was pretty awesome. We went to famous restaurants where I celeb-spotted, and bars (like the famous Sky bar with amazing views of the city) where I saw and smiled at a few famous Hollywood personalities, whose names it would be tacky to drop here. But I also got to know Emilio a little bit better – and can report that he really is the kindest, most down-to-earth person I've met. He appeared genuinely interested in people, with a journalist's desire to tell real stories about authentic people and true-life events as opposed to lightweight commercial entertainment. Both movies he wrote and directed – *The War at Home* (1996), which received great reviews but little play, and the hugely acclaimed movie *Bobby* (2006), about assassinated US Senator Robert F Kennedy – were movies dealing with socio-historic issues.

I have fond memories of hanging out at his house in Malibu discussing our life, death and everything in between – and discovering not only were we the same age, but also knew all the words to the Piña Colada song, which we sang as a duet ...

Sadly, nothing came of the movie as the script was simply horrible – and Emilio had enough nous to understand it was important to get it right or not do it at all – unlike other small-time directors who had a dismal bash at the story a few years later.

I then spent six weeks in the States before returning home to face a possible divorce and to decide what the hell I would do with the rest of my life. I was consumed by the hopelessness of being deeply in love with someone who, when straight and sober, was a caring and inspiring partner with multiple talents. And even though he'd only relapsed briefly a few times and had quickly bounced back, the terror of waiting for the next relapse was destined to hang over me, tainting our life together.

I went to Mexico with a group of Hollywood acquaintances, pottered around Washington, staying in a dive in Foggy Bottom, and then flew back to South Africa. Having rented my Killarney apartment out, I had no reason to move back to Johannesburg, so I took myself off to Durban for a while to stay with family – but I was deeply depressed. My family was understandably not that keen that I brought my chaos and problems to their part of the country, so I soon pottered aimlessly back to Johannesburg to think of what to do next, missing Steven like crazy. All I could think about was how deep our connection had been most of the time, his big laugh and boisterous spirit, and how with him, everything seemed possible. Somehow living without him seemed worse than death.

"Don't phone him," my best friend Wendy said.

I was staying at her place and she was undergoing a bitter divorce so she had some insight into broken hearts.

"Make no contact unless through lawyers."

I couldn't help it. I phoned Steven the third day I was in Johannesburg. No answer. I phoned again. No answer. So I phoned his family to try to track him down. They, in a bid to protect him, wouldn't tell me where he was or give me any information about him at all. They just said they didn't know where he was. So I left a message on Steven's mobile phone. An hour later, he called me back. He was in a government-sponsored rehab in Johannesburg's city centre – certainly a far cry from the fancy Riverfield Lodge where he'd been table tennis champ a few years before.

We agreed to meet the next day when he got out.

"Don't meet with him, Monica," Wendy said. "Think this through properly. You are not being sensible."

I couldn't help it. I walked into a bar in Rosebank. R.E.M.'s "Everybody Hurts" played in the background. I looked over at this dishevelled man in his torn leather jacket and baggy jeans falling off his bum – my gorgeous Steven. So that was it. We were back together, and before the night was out, more enamoured than ever before. We spent the whole night trying to bash out ways to move forward together, trying to figure out how we went from being completely together one minute, to contemplating divorce the next. When we met, we came from very different experiences and upbringings, and our attitudes to many important things were so incredibly different. Being together meant both of us had to make huge changes – but fortunately, changes we agreed we were both willing to make – and that is why in the end love won.

By morning, we had decided to relocate to Nelspruit – far away from the evil Johannesburg with its druggie temptations – to start again, running from Gauteng in search of an improved quality of life.

Chapter 12

Mpumalanga has to be one of the most beautiful places in South Africa, with magnificent scenery, tribal legends, gold-rush mystique and a grand plethora of mighty mountains, imposing passes, dramatic valleys and winding rivers. The true pioneering spirit of the area sucked us right in and we were certainly not the only Gauteng 'refu-flees' seeking greener pastures and new horizons.

On our first day in town, we found an awesome place to stay – a multicultural digs in a Van der Merwe Street subdivided house – with a delightful Christian Indian couple on one side, a single Afrikaner mum and her three teenage kids on the other, an adorable black couple and their two-year-old son and a gay gardener who quickly developed a crush on Steven. Should we have been thrown into despair or depression, the LifeLine Crisis Centre conveniently operated from a cottage on the premises. Once, when Steven was away for a night on an assignment, I took a few sleeping tablets and fell asleep while mid-sentence on a routine phone call to my mother-in-law Tana, who panicked and called LifeLine. The volunteer on duty saw me asleep and called the ambulance. I woke up in hospital, very surprised.

Life was idyllic. We awoke to the shrieks of the purple-crested loeries, the Piet-my-vrous and endless hadedas and hoopoes in our luscious garden. Our days were spent working on a wide variety of interesting stories with a wide assortment of publications. Every evening we would walk into town to the post office hand in hand to check out whether any freelance cheques had arrived for us. When a pay day arrived, we'd walk to the Ocean Basket and order fish and chips with piles of garlic on the side, and we'd share a bottle of wine, me spritzering generously with soda. Sometimes, on seriously hot Lowveld summer days, our only respite from the heat was the local bottle store where we would meet our friends in the beer fridge for sundowners.

When we arrived in town, the only gym was a tiny aerobic studio with a delightfully eccentric owner-instructor who would often forget her routines. Steven and I would regularly attend classes together, until the older women complained that Steven didn't wear undies and they could clearly see his wobbly bits through his flimsy cotton shorts. He joined a squash league instead.

Steven cooked a lot, experimenting with different dishes, and took a part-time job as kitchen hand and chef in White River. He wasn't paid much and the restaurant owner (and main chef) – a gay guy who suddenly decided to marry a woman – was temperamental, and there were scenes of fish being flung at staff, general abuse and vile language. Steven realised the high stress of getting food out fast – and definitely no drinking on the job – wasn't fun. So he would cook for our quirky dinner parties, gathering up arbitrary people we'd just met and wanted to know better. Some parties were a success, others were just awkward.

Round the corner from us was a well-known Mpumalanga artist – known to some as Johnny Golightly (after Holly Golightly in *Breakfast at Tiffany's*), a flamboyant character with a wicked sense of humour and equally delightful parents. At that time, he was living at the back of his dad's house in a converted shed, which Johnny transformed into a creative wonderland.

At one dinner party in Johnny's shed, the rain was so loud on the corrugated-iron roof we couldn't hear each other speak. Our invited guests – a group of arbitraries thrown together in a rather cavalier fashion – clearly didn't appreciate our avant-garde style: the toilet paper for napkins, the mismatched crockery and drunk cook. They sat in prim and shocked silence while Steven, Johnny and I laughed and danced outside in the warm rain.

When we got to Nelspruit, Johnny was recovering from an accident in which he had broken both his ankles jumping out of a hotel window, fleeing some homophobic men he'd met in the hotel bar in a *dorpie* in what was then known as the northern Transvaal.

We loved visiting Johnny and his dad, Willie, who was a warm and generous man with such a quirky and youthful personality. His mum lived with another woman nearby and we shared loads of laughs with that side of the family too. We adopted Johnny's family – mum, dad and mum-in-law (so to speak) as our own – and Willie would often cook us up huge breakfasts and lend us R10 or so for petrol when we were seriously broke (which was often!).

Another memorable occasion was Princess Di's funeral. Naturally, Johnny and I wept to hear of her death – and we dressed up for the funeral in our finest gear – pearls, gloves, long dresses and general gorgeousness. Then we drank loads of sparkling wine (too poor for Champagne!) and ate cucumber sandwiches. We later fell out with Johnny – I think Steven and I were really too loud and bouncy and overpowering on a long-term basis while Johnny was struggling to find a comfortable place in his life – and spent our last six months in Nelspruit living 500 metres apart from Johnny and childishly not talking!

In our few years in Nelspruit, a shopping centre was built, along with a large brand-name gym. The opening of the Riverside Mall made us feel quite cosmopolitan. It was the kind of place you were sure to meet a dozen or more friends and acquaintances every visit. Friday afternoons we'd hang out and drink Long Island ice teas before staggering home. We'd also head up the road to the Bagdad Café in White River every weekend where the food was sublime, the company suitably crazy and always people we knew. The locals were unique. Living away from big cities, most of them had grown up with no idea of social norms so everyone born and bred in Mpumalanga lived life way out of the box. As opposed to city folk, your everyday Lowvelder seemed uninhibited by pretentious social norms with little interest in being 'cool' or 'trendy', and certainly had no inclination towards polite false posturing. For Steven and me, it was a relief to be accepted for who we were, and away from the judgmental critique of the city's conformist police.

One Sunday morning Steven and I were chatting to a group of middle-aged women enjoying a breakfast in a coffee shop at the Bagdad Café and playing my favourite game of "What's in your Handbag?". One by one, we emptied our handbags to display what they contained. One conservatively dressed woman, who had just come from church, pulled out her purse containing, amongst other stuff, a piece of foil.

"What's in the foil?" I asked.

She opened it up and it was a couple of microdots (LSD).

"I like to take a little acid on Sunday as you *know* how boring Sunday lunch with my husband is," she said.

Another woman then confessed that she and her husband had recently tried dope stolen from a stash they found belonging to their 20-year-old son.

"It made the news hilarious; I laughed so much I fell off my chair," she said.

We meticulously divided the microdots and had a very giggly morning with a bunch of fabulously original new friends. Only I seemed deeply surprised and it still rates as one of my most bizarre brunches.

We went to interview a couple of chilli farmers one day for a story we were doing for *Farmer's Weekly* and were met at the door with a couple of butterscotch schnapps. We stayed for lunch and when it came time for sundowners, the hostess was under the table, fast asleep. The following month, we attended her eldest son's wedding, where she whipped off her top, then stomped and danced until the erected dance floor collapsed. Nobody seemed in the slightest bit uptight or shocked and everyone enjoyed themselves enormously.

Our stories were some of the most interesting I've ever done. One minute we were in the Matsulu township writing about a deaf-mute boy who spent eight years tied to an avocado tree as he was mentally unwell and cared for only by an elderly grandma. The next, we covered a cholera epidemic alongside the Lomati River in the Phiva village outside Malelane (now Malalane) near the Kruger National Park. While the river looked like something out of a picture book on the scenic splendour of South Africa, its tranquil beauty threatened death throughout the area. A day later, I was flying over the Blyde River Canyon in a microlight, 1 600 metres above sea level, over Kowyns Pass and the Mac Mac Falls on one side and Mozambique away in the distance. Our animal stories included a woman who survived a hippo attack, Frikkie the lonely rhino who kept flattening zebras by trying to mate with them, a couple who kept mongooses as pets, and endless tales of lions and crocodiles on the rampage. We also wrote about entrepreneurs selling African Love Dust made of verdite and a group of factory workers who made and polished wooden penises that were then used for sex education. We met Queen Modjaji, the Rain Queen; danced with Nelson Mandela at the opening of a community centre; watched boxing at the Barberton Correctional Services and went to learn the *sakkie dans* and the waltz at Tollie's "Love Is" Dance Studio.

Nelspruit is the gateway to Zimbabwe, Mozambique and Swaziland so Steven and I were spoilt with places to adventure to. Getting across borders always proved tricky, mainly because of corruption and the extortion of bribes. On one occasion, we were trying to get into Mozambique via the Espungabera border post via Zimbabwe. We checked through the friendly Zimbabwean post and had to travel eight kilometres to Mozambique. On arriving there, they shook their heads and looked threatening. We were told to drive 500 kilometres back to Harare.

While officials spoke to each other in English, they only communicated with us in Portuguese. Dusty and hot, we wondered if we were expected to pay a bribe. We sat. They ignored us. Then a price was settled on. We had to pay for extra 'administration' which they were able to complete on the spot – and we were let in.

On other trips, we were stopped for not having our three red triangles in Mozambique, for overtaking on a white line on a rural track (no lines at all obvious) and often for speeding. There was always something. I seethed. Steven paid.

As Nelspruit is only two and a half hours from Manzini, in Swaziland, we'd head off to visit every couple of months. At first, we would cover activities happening at the Swazi Sun and other popular resorts. Then we spent time documenting the colourful Swazi Umhlanga Reed Festival where thousands of virgin girls with bare breasts and swaying hips were paraded in front of King Mswati the Third, the royal family, which included his many wives, dignitaries, cabinet ministers, locals and tourists. A coming-of-age ritual for maidens of marriageable age, the festival started four days previously when the young maidens gathered reeds from the Isuthu River outside Manzini and lay them at the Queen Mother's home in the Ezulweni River. On the back of this work, Steven got a commission from the Swazi Tourism Board to photograph the country, so we spent a few months in and out of that glorious little country.

Steven also had a stimulating commission documenting the new highway linking the corridor between Johannesburg and Maputo in Mozambique. From Nelspruit, it was about an hour to the border, then another two or three hours to get to the capital of Maputo, depending on the queue at the border. His brief was to document the people and industries along the route and then exhibit the pictures to promote the project to the public and inform rural locals in a way that crossed language barriers. It was a fairly low-budget affair and intended to be relaxed and informal, with pictures ranging from humorous human pictures, interesting industrial insights, signage and people mixed with stunning panoramic pictures, insights into agriculture and everything in between.

It was hugely successful at grassroot level and Steven exhibited it many times – always simply laminating pictures and sticking them up in very public places. He launched his exhibition in the centre of Nelspruit, hanging his pictures with pegs on a steel wash line. He involved the local buskers, including, ironically, a blind singer, and the flamboyant Department of Arts and Recreation director, Jerry Mofokeng, opened it.

We'd been in Mpumalanga for not even a year when Steven got a summons from the Tax Department. He'd not done his taxes for the past eight years. So we got him all up to date. Within the month, he'd got a lovely tax return.

"London's calling," he said.

So we took off for three weeks and this time we went via Egypt. On the banks of the River Nile this glittering African city was for us a wacky mix of ancient and modern, East and West. As we got off our bus at our modest hotel, the touts swarmed like locusts, trying to take us to a "much better place, very clean, very cheap".

Later, we slunk out to buy food. But our escape did not go undetected. While buying take-away kebabs and coffee from a local vendor, a stranger took it upon himself to 'assist' us with the food order.

Before we knew what had happened, he'd picked up our food and we were following his lead, chasing our food through cars and people while he chatted away to us non-stop.

"My name is Karim and you are very welcome here. Where are you from? Let me show you around. You staying somewhere good, somewhere clean? Very please to meet you."

We ended up at the factory of his 'uncle' who brought out a platter of sweetmeats and glasses of cola and tried to sell us perfume and carpets.

I had to practically wrestle Steven to the floor and roll him out the door when he was overwhelmed with their persistent and ruthless sales tactics. Then we both sprinted for freedom, leaving our food behind.

"From now on, make no eye contact with anyone in this city, ya' hear?" I said. "Leave all talking to me ... you're just too bloody friendly."

Fed up with being hassled so much by hustlers trying to make a buck off us, we slunk out of our hotel the next morning and headed off to the least touristy area, often getting hopelessly lost in the labyrinth of filthy side streets in the old Cairo.

Instead of visiting the Antiquities Museum and the Pyramids as planned, we explored the ancient suburbs of the old city. We walked past old men in djellaba robes sitting in coffee shops playing chess, into dim-lit, narrow streets teeming with chickens, goats and children. Through the maze-like back alleys littered with festering garbage, we discovered colourful bazaars with a treasure trove of delights. On every corner was a glittering minaret atop the many beautifully tiled mosques where men bowed and kneeled towards Mecca as the muezzin intoned the Koran.

Steven paused to enjoy a leisurely sheesha, the bubble pipe full of flavoured tobacco, while I sat and drank coffee through cubes of sugar, watching the people walk by and soaking in this curious African-Arabic culture.

From there, we went on to visit our old favourite – London – spending time with Steven's long-time fabulous friend from his Rhodes University days, Nigel Stephen Wrench, who is always good for a great time. But it was equally gorgeous to head back to the Lowveld again – the first time we'd holidayed and had something to go back to.

Six months later, Steven gave up smoking – again – so, irritated with his bad temper, I phoned my oldest and close friend, Debbie, whom I have known now for nearly 45 years.

"Let's go to London together," I said. "Like we talked about when we were teenagers."

Within hours, we'd booked our flights for the following Saturday.

Steven organised me a lift to Johannesburg to catch my flight. The lift arrived – two incredibly drunk gay boys with cut-off pink vests and day-glo pants driving a Bantam bakkie. I jumped in the back with my enormous suitcase, where I snuggled down next to an equally drunk girl who spent the entire trip rolling over on me, singing sex-driven pop songs to me.

She'd then stop to take a big gulp of *brandewyn*, followed by a massive burp. Then she'd start the song again. Meanwhile, the boys were shooting at road signs out the window with a shotgun and screaming with high-pitched delight.

A hundred kilometres out of Johannesburg, the bakkie hit a massive bump, smashed the sump and the vehicle could go no further. I hitched a lift to the next petrol station and called my brother from a pay phone to fetch me.

"I've had a few drinks ... I'm in a pub," he said.

"No problem," I wept. "Fetch me now ... my life depends on it."

Debbie and I had a hilariously good girlie time in London with lots of shopping and comedy clubbing and shows. We walked all day, talked continuously, laughed and explored until we were exhausted, and it was heart-warming to see one of my favourite cities through the eyes of someone who had not visited before.

But when I arrived back in Johannesburg, Steven met me with flowers and demands that I never, ever leave him on holiday again.

"I've given up cigarettes," he said. "But I've taken up cigars."

Debbie was really keen to return home to her husband and three children, whereas I still had given no thought to children at all, bar the Aids orphans I was now regularly coming into contact with.

I was becoming increasingly aware of the children caught up in the Aids pandemic sweeping the country in the '90s. As a WASP princess I tended to be more attracted to the trivial and glamorous, picking my 'ag shame' cases a little further from heart and home.

But then I met two little girls, orphaned by Aids and dying of the disease. At the time I was investigating a story about a municipality that had cut off lights and water to an informal foster home because of unpaid bills. The foster mother, Sophie Jardim, had been left in the dark, with no hot water and a dozen needy babies to bathe, clothe and fed. When I met these two little girls, they were skeletal – grey and emaciated, lying side by side on a bed, whimpering weakly. I picked them up, and they were both so cold. I returned a week later with blankets and food, but one of the little girls had already died. The other died a few weeks later.

I was devastated. However, I knew that when children are born with Aids, their mothers are often dying from the disease, so the parents had neither the strength nor resources to care for the children. It was left to the overworked and understaffed social workers to try to place the children. I became increasingly involved with stories covering informal orphanages popping up across the Mpumalanga Province to cope with the ravages of the pandemic. Because we were close to Zimbabwe, Swaziland and Mozambique,

Nelspruit was central to the trucking route that spread the disease. The area therefore became a prime spot for children orphaned by Aids. Many of these children were not South African as their parents were illegal immigrants and they therefore had no extended family and received no government support. Many people were not willing to take in Aids babies, especially those without South African birth certificates, because it meant no government child-care grants and they required 24-hour nursing. It was up to white women on a mission to care for them, and Steven and I befriended a few such people running informal orphanages.

Steven was still very involved with his Maputo Corridor project and the exhibition was growing in popularity. We hung it in Parliament in Cape Town and in the corridors of the Union Buildings in Pretoria. We took it to an enormous gallery in Maputo; it was hung at the border post at Komatipoort, and on the walls of shopping centres from Joburg to Maputo. Steven was really happy. He was really healthy and content. He was basically a country boy at heart and loved our balance between city and small-town living. I spent more time than I wanted putting pictures up and taking them down, not always very happy because I missed Johannesburg's man-made energy.

Three years later, I got itchy feet again and longed to return to a city. I felt like everyone else was having a fabulous time in the 'real' world and I was rotting away in the sticks. I whinged and whined and begged and sulked and pleaded. So we went to Durban – home of Point Road and crack cocaine.

Chapter 13

From one tropical climate to another, our Durban experience was infused with vibrant colours and the heady scent of frangipanis and bougainvillea, spices and hot tar. In an African city with a massive Zulu population, mosques and bazaars sit alongside temples and wildly coloured deities, next to Victorian buildings and African markets. The delightful cacophony of culture was a source of constant delight to us both.

Our tenth-floor apartment on the Berea Ridge looked over the city down to the sea. We set up the dining-room table along the massive front window and spent hours sitting there, looking out at the beautiful world outside. Surrounded by mosques a few roads back, our days were regulated by the deeply moving muezzin's call to prayer blown in by the Ridge winds.

We moved into our apartment a week before the end of 1999. Sitting in our apartment on New Year's Eve, we wondered how we would mark the momentous occasion of the start of a new century (or the end of the old one depending on where you stood on semantics). Steven's old friend, Michael Markovitz, was holding a party with others in Cape Town and he called to ask us about our New Year's plans. Steven looked at me. I looked at him. Then, with no money in our current account, we bought two tickets on a credit card and jumped on the last plane out of town. Another close friend, Andrew Meintjies, picked us up at the airport, and within a few hours, we'd gone from sitting in our apartment in Durban to a shindig in Cape Town partying with two of Steven's favourite people. As dawn broke, Steven and I were on the first flight home again.

Life in Durban was free and easy. We could be seen in the local gym most mornings working out together, singing along to the aerobics music and throwing in a few groovy dance moves of our own. We joined the early-morning beach walk brigade nearly every day and took up body boarding. Steven was in curry heaven and we'd often wander down to Grey Street (as it was then known) to pick up a spicy dish or two, or walk down to the race track where the restaurant sold a mean curry. Personally, I still don't understand what is attractive about eating food that burns before and after, but I was just glad Steven was cheerful. Naturally, we gathered a new assortment of interesting and artistic odd-bods from all walks of life, inviting lovely people over for very laid-back and dishevelled dinner parties. Steven continued to drink more than he cooked so often the food wasn't the star of the show.

Weekends offered open-air concerts at the Botanical Gardens among the orchids, ferns, cycads and bromelias, braais at Kings Park after watching the Sharks play, hikes through Oribi Gorge on the South Coast, innovative Red Eye events at the Durban Art Gallery and Durban Symphonic Orchestra concerts in the glorious old Town Hall. Our life was a beautiful balance between culture and sport, nature and home, The Pavilion and Musgrave Centre, work and play.

I was delighted to get a job on Independent Newspapers and then Steven soon followed as a photographer. We loved working together and certainly were quite loud, but the newsroom staff were so friendly and tolerant, amused by our puppy-like enthusiasm for the Durban experience.

There were so many new places to explore and write stories about together and our trusty white Toyota Corolla clocked impressive mileage travelling through the rolling green hills of the Midlands to the dramatic Drakensberg mountains, up past the

North Coast sugar-cane fields to Hluhluwe Game Reserve, down the South Coast to the Transkei border and even time indulging in a little sightseeing in Newcastle, Dundee and Estcourt, home of the Park Pie.

I loved being part of a community at work again, snuggling down with other journalists and photographers to put together newspapers. However, my love of hard news had waned and I found myself far more interested in writing feature stories. I'd loved freelancing with Steven in the first few years of our marriage. Writing news – researching and presenting facts – is fairly simple and routine, whereas compiling an interesting 2 000–3 000-word article appealed to my more chatty writing style. So, even though I loved the vibe of the newspaper, after a year, I jumped at a job offer as resident writer in Durban for *Fairlady* magazine, working from home.

At first, my days were spent blissfully at my desk, looking out of my aforementioned window, researching and writing morning to night. But as the year passed, I became lonely as I had nobody to interact much with face to face during the working day. Steven continued having fun at work at the newspaper down the road, and it made me feel left out and isolated. I started to miss the social interaction and structure of a newsroom. I needed to bounce ideas off people, feed off others' ideas and opinions, plus a reason to get out of my pyjamas. But all day, there was just me, the fridge and my desk.

Furthermore, our weekends weren't all about sunshine, surf and bunny chows. The dark and sinister side started to encroach on our island of happiness: the dodgy Point Road drug scene right near the Durban harbour, a major international port and transport hub. We were very, very careful not to go there for the first six months. But then, of course, the lure was too great so we'd occasionally forage into the local drug dens, the Lonsdale Hotel and Point Road nightclubs, where we would buy drugs and get trashed.

Gone were the days of my teenage youth where I would lounge round the Lonsdale Hotel pool at lunchtimes on Sunday listening to cover bands play Lionel Richie, Bob Seger, Neil Young and Lou

Reed hits instead of staying at the beach where my parents thought I was. Now it had become a crack den teeming with well-built African immigrants draped in gold chains, drug addicts and prostitutes.

Because there was little coke powder around, which was expensive, and lots and lots of crack, which was cheap, we'd sometimes go overboard and our lives careered out of control.

While crack proved neither recreation nor fun, the thought of the incredible rush was frighteningly addictive and I had begun to understand how easy it was to get hooked. Fortunately for me, Steven had spent the last few years together rebuilding his confidence and love of life, establishing himself as an interesting and vital photographer where friends and colleagues valued his quirky eye and natural energy. And that became more important to him than drugs.

But I, always looking for adventure and fun, was still up for a walk on the wild side. After one horrible night where I'd pulled Steven along into chasing a high, I awoke with a massive hangover and we both realised we were surfing too close to toppling over the edge into serious chaos.

I knew my druggie days were over. I'd dipped my toes in that putrid pond and found it far too demeaning and frightening. We didn't even discuss it. We just knew: no more. Our lives were better than that. I certainly never did any so-called recreational drugs again and, to my knowledge, neither did Steven. It was absolutely and utterly a road we'd travelled to its end.

Fortunately, our super-healthy lifestyle and sense of genuine fun pulled us quickly back on track with little damage done … but I knew I would never be smug about sobriety again. It was a tiny part of our wonderful Durban experience, yet one that haunts me still.

However, we survived it together – and remained deeply in love, very tight, very united – two bodies, two brains and one vision.

Six months later, I was offered a position as Bureau Chief of *Fairlady* magazine in Johannesburg. I felt torn, because I'd ripped Steven away from the Lowveld, which he loved, and was now talking about moving back to Johannesburg, just as he was settled and perfectly happy in Durban. But since the drug issue felt resolved, I felt safe to return to a city with the creative and inspirational energy I truly adore.

"What do you think?" I asked him.

"Let's go," he replied.

So once again, these Hilton-Barbers were packing up and moving.

Chapter 14

I didn't really think much about having children. It was something I vaguely planned maybe sometime in the future. Then I turned 37 years old and BOOM. My biological clock kicked me hard in the head. In fact, the need to breed hit me with such powerful force, I felt ill with desperate longing.

I didn't even know I liked children until Steven and I lived in Nelspruit and covered stories on the growing number of Aids orphans in the area. After spending a few hours a week helping out in informal foster homes, fund-raising, caring for children and generally hanging about, I fell in love with the little people.

Steven used to call me Poppet or Poppet Pie and the little ones, for whom English was a second language, misunderstood. So when my favourites – four boys aged between six and eight years old – ran out to greet us with outstretched arms, they yelled: "It's the Puppy Pies … the Puppy Pies are here."

I adored going there for the love given to us in return for our interest in them. Steven was so sweet with them, swinging them round, acting like a clown and dispensing tickles and cuddles indiscriminately.

But still, family seemed some future dream. Even though I was no spring chicken, I still felt far too young to tie myself down to motherhood. For some unfathomable reason, I never worried about being too old to start a family. But I had definitely not made the decision NOT to have a family.

Then in early 2001, in a phone conversation with my mother, she said: "You made a sensible decision not to have any children, what with your lifestyle and personality."

Kapow.

I was suddenly filled with an indescribable yearning for my own snuffly bundle of creation. Steven was right on board.

Of course, he thought it would take me a year or so to fall pregnant, not because of my age but because I had been on the pill for nearly two decades. As luck would have it, I was pregnant a month after I went off the pill – a frickin' miracle – a few months into starting my new job as Bureau Chief at *Fairlady* magazine in Johannesburg. Yip, how embarrassing was that! Fortunately, the then editor, Alice Bell, could not have been more supportive and encouraging. As a mum of three herself, she had taken time out of her career to raise children, and was professionally charming despite my poor timing.

We were staying in this tiny little apartment off Katherine Street in Rivonia overlooking a major petrol station. We used to have a little bucket which we would hang out the window with money in. We'd lower it down our wall and call out to one of the attendants in the forecourt, who would grab the bucket through the fence, run into the shop and buy whatever was on our list – usually bread or milk – then put it back in our bucket and we would pull it back up again. It was glorious fun and we were giddy with the excitement of being back in Johannesburg. Both of us were really healthy, going off to gym every day and keeping to a clean diet. Steven had given up cigarettes and even his alcoholic beverages were few and far between.

The minute my period was late, I went off to buy a pregnancy kit without telling Steven. If the news was good – hard to believe as it was too soon – I imagined organising a candle-lit dinner and gift-wrapping the pregnancy test with a pair of baby bootees. Instead, I was so excited, I hopped out of the bathroom, panties round my ankles, yelling: "Woo HOO. We're going to have a baby!" Steven turned yellow-white and was quiet for an hour or so, but I was bouncing about and yabbing away enough for both of us. And Steven soon pinked up and joined in my head-over-heels joy and delight.

As the months rolled by, Steven and I were beyond excited. He was the perfect expectant father, growing in sympathy as big as me, making endless healthy meals. I didn't just eat for two. I ate for an entire family. I grew. Steven grew. We'd put our tummies together – and it was a magnificent sight. Eggs on toast, freshly squeezed orange juice, meals delivered to the office for me, delicious suppers, flowers constantly, I was treated like the first woman ever to have a baby, like a precious jewel. Steven would walk in front of me in public, cutting a smooth path, protecting me and my stomach from crowds. We went to baby classes together and laughed our way through. I didn't pay one dot of notice to the natural birthing sections as I always intended to have at least an epidural with as many drugs as staff would give me. Steven massaged my feet, stroked my back, brushed my hair and put up with my fatty-boom-boom grumps.

And in all of this, I was blissfully happy at work where my colleagues were swept along in my baby fever. But, like many pregnant women, I was prone to crying. Steven and I went back to Nelspruit to cover a story about a woman giving Aids tests to children who had been raped. We spent a day trailing around with her, watching her take blood from two little girls, aged three and four, who had been repeatedly raped by a man in their community who was reported to have Aids. Only a few days previously, the woman told us about visiting an 18-month-old baby in hospital, a child who soon died of injuries due to extensive damage to internal organs following a brutal rape. The baby was split top to toe and ripped apart. Steven and I wept. We sobbed so hard on the trip home to Johannesburg, we had to stop halfway for a cup of rooibos tea (me) and mega-strong sweet, black coffee (Steven) to pull ourselves together. When I went into the office to write up the story, I cried more. For the rest of my pregnancy, I avoided tragic baby stories.

Steven hosted and catered for my baby shower in his usual enthusiastic and messy style – loads of food and happiness and me waddling round in a short red-and-yellow daisy-patterned dress like a bright and fabulous heffalump. By now, we'd bought an enormous three-bedroom flat in a small Illovo building overlooking Wanderers Cricket Grounds with mega-high ceilings, lots of elderly Jewish people fighting over parking spaces and one seldom-seen affluent black lawyer who bought but never bothered to move in properly. So neighbours, friends and family crowded into our flat one sunny afternoon in late November 2001, with gifts and good wishes. I was surrounded by people I loved.

My office also organised a baby shower for me. Due to general pregnancy fatigue and hypertension, I left work a month before my due date. My beautiful *Fairlady* co-workers secretly decorated the office and told me I had to come in for a meeting with Alice Bell. They had organised food, presents, made posters and stuck them all over the walls. I nearly spoilt it all by arriving too early and saw them pottering around, wondering what the hell was going on, before wandering off to return a bit later. But my baby brain was so soft, I didn't realise, even after the party, that there was in fact no actual meeting! It was only when I asked about when the meeting started – and everyone looked at me in surprise – that I realised NO MEETING, just an excuse to get me there for the party – ha ha! One of the marketing ladies, Dominique Hayes, who had children herself, predicted I would be having my baby very, very soon, despite not being due for over three weeks. The next day, my waters broke.

As is the way of many couples expecting a baby very soon, I was uncomfortable and crabby. Steven was snoring. So I huffed off to the spare room for the night, only to wake up finding myself peeing in the bed. Except when I stood up, I was still peeing. So, flinging off my sodden panties, I shuffled down the corridor.

"Wake up, wake up," I yelled at the sleeping Steven.

Steven sat bolt upright in bed, his thick, wild hair standing up and eyes round in fright.

"Something's wrong," I cried.

Steven looked at the puddle on the floor and said: "Oh my god, oh my god, your waters have broken."

I was bewildered. Steven panicked. Steven phoned the hospital, who said to come right on in. We rushed about packing bags. And Steven drove in a daze.

The timing was not great because it was the final day of South Africa's first *Big Brother* series – and the programme was hugely popular. Steven was the *Big Brother* photographer so 9 December 2001 was a big day for him as pictures had to be taken and syndicated around the world. It was the culmination of months of work. Pulling another photographer in at this late stage would have been very difficult.

Secondly, I still had a clitoris piercing Steven and I thought seemed a good idea a few years ago – and we hadn't thought to take it out yet. So we arrived at the hospital, excited and nervous, and the examining nurse took one look at the piercing and started giggling. She told us it had to come out pronto. Steven was so nervous, and with his clumsy and shaking hands, he tried to take the ring out. But the fastener must have 'glued' tightly shut, and he wasn't deft enough to unscrew it. After fiddling and faffing around, then a few frustrated tugs and pulls, Steven was not winning. So our very kind but conservative gynaecologist – a gentle lanky man called Lou Pistorius – found a pair of steel clippers and cut it off. We were already the talk of the Sandton Clinic. We waited all day, but I never went into labour, so by late afternoon, it was C-section time. I wasn't one dot afraid of labour pains, and surprisingly, gave no thought to it at all. I was just incredibly elated to be having a baby. I didn't care how the child came out. I just wanted to have my baba in my arms. Steven took pictures while I quivered with anticipation.

"Right, let's go," Dr Pistorius said. He helped push me into the operating theatre. And within 10 minutes, Benjamin was born. Steven, overwhelmed by the process, hid behind the camera and took pictures. Like so many new mums, I was so thrilled I could hardly contain myself. When I held Benjamin in my arms, I was shocked at how powerful my love was for this stunning baby with his pouty mouth, black eyes and deep dimples. He was my mini-Steven.

"When can we have our next one," I said to Steven and Dr Pistorius as I left the operating clinic.

"Hold up … give it a year," Dr Pistorius laughed.

I wasn't totally happy though.

Steven insisted on having Benjamin circumcised like he was. It was partially some allegiance to African circumcision rituals, plus his belief that it was cleaner and healthier. We were unable to resolve it and while I was asleep, Benjamin was circumcised. When I saw his mutilated penis later that day, I felt like the worst mother in the world and I was momentarily plunged into post-baby blues.

"How could you?" I cried.

"But you didn't say no properly … I thought you meant yes," Steven replied.

I felt like I had failed to protect Benjamin.

I was also unhappy in the crowded ward. Despite asking for a private room, overcrowding meant I had to share with a group of rather bitchy women who sniggered at my brash over-enthusiasm. I know not everyone is comfortable with my intensity but I was feeling ultra-sensitive and took their mean comments, overheard during visiting hours, badly – that I had snored during the night, that I was too loud and like Tigger on amphetamines. I cried my heart out and demanded to be moved into a private room … only for the nurses to play a trick on me. When I went to the baby ward to fetch my day-old newborn, they hid him and pretended he had been stolen. To be fair, because Steven and I had been so full of laughter and jokes they never imagined I would take it so badly and for them, it was playful teasing. But I was so freaked out, I was convinced the staff were evil and were really going to steal my boy and I phoned Steven to demand he collect me immediately. Unfortunately, Steven was holding a head-wetting party at our home and was less than keen – for once not very supportive, which *does* now in retrospect make me wonder what the hell was actually going on – so I had to wait until morning to get out of there. Steven arrived the following morning, looking very hungover and rumpled.

We drove home with our Benjamin at about 30 kilometres an hour, stunned at how fast and carelessly people on the roads drove, terrified of having an accident.

Our early days of parenthood were bliss, us and our baby. Steven carried Ben around in the palm of his hand, getting up to bring Baby for his feeds and doing the burping and nappy changes and caring for me. The only hiccough was his increasing jealousy of my love for my family and his resentment of the bond I had with my parents, Gail and siblings. He wanted me to make him and Benjamin my only family – whereas having a baby meant I wished to have my family around more than ever.

I wanted Benjamin christened because I wanted him to wear the christening dress my grandmother had lovingly made for my eldest brother when he was born and passed down through all four of us siblings, and then onto our children. Like me and my brothers and sisters and our children, I wanted Ben to be baptised by my dad in the same church font we had all been baptised in. Steven didn't. However, since the circumcision debacle, Steven was well out of bargaining chips. I attended christening classes at St Thomas's church in Johannesburg where I occasionally took Benjamin, and we went down to the Pietermaritzburg Cathedral for the christening. Benjamin's godparents included a gay artist from Mpumalanga, Johnny (unfortunately battling his own demons and unable attend), Steven's Jewish best friend, Michael Markovitz (clearly this was merely in spirit only!) and Andrew Meintjies, a beloved friend we both adored. Gail, my dad's wife, was godmother. Steven took so many pictures, my younger sister Lucy was stiffly outraged as she thought Steven was treating it as a photo opportunity rather than a religious event. Then we returned to Gail's and Dad's home in Pietermaritzburg and enjoyed lunch, cake and a little wine. Andrew, who had driven all the way down from Johannesburg for the event, sat outside on the lawn with our family, chatting and sunning his curly-headed self. After he set off back to the Big Smoke, Steven wanted to lie down for an afternoon nap, a concept that annoyed my family since we are more of the "Let's go for a long walk" than "a nap would be good" folk. So, all in all, Benjamin's christening was a typical family celebration.

Two months later, Steven was dead.

Chapter 15

Life in the H-B household was sailing along very smoothly. I was back working at *Fairlady* and Steven was very happy freelancing and exhibiting his Maputo Corridor project and pictures from the Bushveld. Everything in our life looked promising. We had savings. Steven had an education fund going for Benjal. We fell more and more in love every day, were already keen for another child, and we were humming along together perfectly on a smooth road to a calm and fulfilling future with only a few bumpy patches to keep it real.

We put our treasured son into a nearby crèche when he was just two months old, and it was agonising. It turned out to be a BIG MISTAKE as he was far too young, and made me feel depressed and guilty. Benjamin became ill from the get-go – and never really regained perfect health. But I was in the Johannesburg mode of work, work, work – and immersed in the typical South African culture where kids go to crèche or stay home with a nanny. Steven had been raised by his nanny, Malea, known also as his 'other mother', whom he loved and stayed in contact with all his adult life, and he wanted the same for Benjamin. But our attempt to find a nanny was unsuccessful. We only interviewed one woman, and she wanted a mobile phone, television in her own room with en-suite bathroom, pension and medical aid, on top of a salary half of mine with food included. For us, this was unaffordable and the thought of sharing my home with another woman didn't make me feel comfortable. Not having 'enjoyed' the luxury of South Africa's privileged lifestyle of live-in or permanent help either growing up or as an adult, I didn't feel that employer role was going to become me.

I thought there would be more checks and balances in a child-care centre. But the first place we sent him felt like an institution with rooms deep down in the basement and only artificial light that was run like a military operation. So we took in a young teenager and gave her board, lodging and tertiary education in exchange for her caring for our son, but she was too young, always hiving off with her boyfriend, and then later fell pregnant. So it was back to day care for him where he went back to being sick and I was overwhelmed with mother-guilt.

Steven was working really hard and finding a groove doing lots of work with a media PR company he adored, eating out lots, trying to keep away from cigarettes, and drinking probably more than was good for him. He was always dashing in and out of home in a hive of activity, clothes flapping and tousled hair flopping. I was focused on our child and work – and Steven, instead of being my Number One and Only Priority, had slipped down to third place.

One day he came into the house and told me a doctor had told him his blood pressure was dangerously high.

"The doc looked shocked … told me to make another appointment to check it out," he said.

Steven had gone to get an injection for his back pain. He'd been a very enthusiastic tennis player in his teen years and had damaged his vertebrae. He'd had to have two lower-back discs fused in his early twenties. But when he spent too much time chasing his tail and not strengthening his back with exercise, his back sometimes seized and caused pain. So he'd gone off one lovely spring day to hunt down a doctor for pain relief after a night of throbbing lower-back pain. In his usual slapdash style, he simply breezed into the nearest and most convenient surgery somewhere around Dunkeld – not one he'd been to before – and waited for a gap. When the doctor did a quick check, he was alarmed at how high his blood pressure was. He also took a cholesterol reading and told Steven that since he'd merely popped in sans appointment, he didn't have time to do a thorough check. But he urged Steven to make another appointment for a thorough medical examination.

"He said if the readings are accurate, I'm on the verge of a heart attack," Steven said.

I looked up at him standing there, slightly pale and breathless, and a wave of worry washed over me.

"Listen up, Steven," I said. "Make the appointment soon … don't just leave it."

Of course, it was put on the 'to-do' list and he never got round to it – and I simply forgot to remind him. Ironically, if that had been me, Steven would have been on my case until the appointment was made, but he took less care of himself. I look back now and wish – if only, we should have, could have … oh, if only.

Over time, the vibe between my family and Steven had become a bit tense. Most of my siblings are madly into sport and health – thanks to my mother's before-her-time attitude to fitness. Steven's massive appetite for drinking, eating and sleeping was kinda annoying for some people – and he could behave like a buffoon on family occasions. Pulled between my family and Steven, I wasn't always the most supportive wife. So when I wanted to take Benjamin to see my dad and Gail, I decided to visit alone.

I left Steven putting up shelving in the spare room in our massive Illovo apartment with his sister Bridget's then husband B, and I flew off to Natal on an autumn Friday afternoon. There were lots of hugs and kisses for Benjy and me, even though we were returning on Sunday. Steven and I talked a few times that night.

"I am really missing you two," he said.

"The flat feels so quiet and empty without you both here."

"I love you both so much."

But the next day, he didn't phone to say good morning. By mid-morning, I was worried. Really frickin' anxious. By lunchtime, I knew something was wrong and started to feel scared. I had left many messages on his phone – and kept leaving messages, which became increasingly irate with fear. Deep down, I knew something was wrong. I imagined he'd gone off on a drug bender – and was in some crack house somewhere trashed out of his mind. Overcome with terror and deep concern, I phoned Bridget, and begged her to just go to our apartment to check if Steven or our car was there.

She took along B. The car was there, but there was no answer to their knocking. So they gained access to the apartment by climbing onto the balcony via the neighbour's balcony. Steven was lying dead on the bed. Once again, my life was to change with a phone call.

"He's gone," she said.

"Gone where?" I replied.

"He's dead."

She was crying so hard, she handed the phone to B, who sounded shocked, but just gave me some details that helped me process that Steven was dead.

He had suffered a heart attack. He was only 39 years old.

A night of partying, an early-morning game of squash and – voilà – all over Red Rover.

The news was so preposterous, I couldn't really take it in. Benjamin had just come out of his bath and was lying on the bed, red and rosy and with the delicious smell of baby soap and powder. As I took the call, Gail stepped in to care for Benjamin while my dad watched me with increasing concern … he could see the news was really bad. At first, the words made no sense. The fact that I had already lost a husband made it too difficult to properly comprehend. Once again, my brain whirred then clouded over and shut down – so much so, I had to go outside and sit alone to try to clear my head. I just wanted quiet to try to let the news sink in. The noise in my head was so loud – all the natural drugs pumping into my system – like my brain was short-circuiting and fuses were blowing left, right and centre causing chaos. I felt like my head was going to explode. But my family were befuddled and hovering in the background, urging me to come inside and care for the child, make arrangements, to phone Steven's mother – and I was paralysed with shock.

The evening was clear and stars were coming out. Tana,

Steven's mother, had also been outside – standing on the veranda outside the family home in the Agatha Valley listening to an owl in a massive tree hooting mournfully. I remember feeling her horror and pain through the phone line, her utter bewilderment – and wondering how she would survive.

I felt so tired.

It was too late to fly home so I had to wait until morning. How I got home, I can't much recall. I lost my boarding ticket – I left it in the toilet before boarding – which caused a problem. However, airline staff found a place for me to sit with Benjamin and, as I took off, my dad and Gail left by car for Johannesburg to arrive only hours after I got home. My brother, Andrew, fetched me from the airport. And after that, it is all mostly a big blur with only a few flashes of recollection.

On arriving home, I heard that while Steven lay dead and family awaited the mortuary van to arrive, someone had stolen Steven's laptop and mobile phone. One minute the items were there, the next his belongings were gone. Incredible! I still wonder who stole his stuff – people from the morgue, the few friends and relatives coming in and out the apartment, or the dodgy neighbours?

The funeral was, for me, mad and hysterical. Memories are fleeting and softly focused. I recall Bridget coming with me to the funeral parlour and looking at the body of Steven, where he was rolled out from a fridge and sensitively arranged for my viewing. The stark reality was crushing. Steven's spirit had gone. Absolutely. All that was left was a white, plastic body – cold to touch – and I felt strangely disconnected. There lay a stranger.

The man who greeted us at the funeral parlour was suitably arranged to exude solemn dignity and respect. He spoke very slowly and in a low voice, reeking of insincere sympathy and fake gravitas while he was selling us coffins, trying to extol the virtues of a large wooden casket lined with purple material, suitable for someone of Steven's length and build. But I was having no bar of it. It was to be a closed-coffin service, he was going directly to be cremated, and I, ever financially cautious, knew I had a young son to be fiscally responsible for.

"Nah," I insisted. "A small box is fine."

"But," the man said, his mournful expression dropping slightly to flash a touch of irritation, "he won't fit. His shoulders are too wide and his legs are too long."

"So chop his arms and feet off and chuck them on top of his body," was my response.

Bridget and I dissolved into helpless, mirthful hysterics and clutched our sides as we staggered our way to the car, with the now thin-lipped and disapproving funeral director looking at us with displeasure.

I have no idea how the funeral parlour resolved the problem of the too-small-and-cheap coffin.

In one way, Steven's death was 'easier' in that I was not alone. I had the full support of his family, who took responsibility for many details like payment and funeral service and wakes. But with grief came a lot of laughter.

I worried about Tana and how she would cope at the funeral. I kept referring to Steven as Ken all the time because, in my head, the dead husband had always been Ken. I treasure the memory of Steven's brother Brett greeting 'friends' at the funeral and thanking them for attending the funeral, only to discover they were not of 'our' party but the previous funeral service, which was leaving as we were all arriving. I giggled at my brother, Simon, recollecting fondly how Steven's pants were always falling down and how the family were always giving him belts as gifts, which he never used. We sang "All Things Bright and Beautiful" in all its seven verses, each followed by a chorus, which was probably longer than many, including me, were expecting. I recall the funeral pall bearers struggling to lift Steven in his coffin into the hearse, and watching the vehicle bump down with a momentous crashing sound over a speed hump as it drove away.

"Good grief," I laughed and laughed madly while clutching onto my friend Poxy Bush. "Steven is still creating a scene even on his way to the morgue."

Sitting in a gutter outside a bar in Melville at the wake, I talked to some coke-head about his post-binge depression, then listened to a man called Casper (oh, the details I remember!) telling me to face grief head on, to stare at it until it dissolved into nothing. I caught up with people I hadn't seen for years and a gathering of wonderful people I really like to hang out with – the Mpumalanga gang, newspaper colleagues, weirdos and arbitraries, and artists and creatives we'd collected along the way. And I knew Steven would have loved to have been there.

My love for my child sheltered and comforted me. He was so like his daddy, with his wide shoulders and stumpy solid little legs, gorgeous black eyes, right down to the childhood asthma ... and his little life carried me upwards and forwards. I only wished I had listened to my third sense, telling me to get out of Johannesburg and chill out, to take me and my baby back to Durban where I would be surrounded by family and a laid-back lifestyle. But I am ashamed to say I was addicted to the Johannesburg vibe and my job – the excitement that anything was possible – and my personal ambition and ego.

So, that was the end of my life with Steven. To this day, I still miss him, his all-embracing love and his positive energy, terribly. He always made me feel like the world was a wonderful place, that fun was around the next corner, and that he would sort out any problem "sharp-sharp like a Minora".

"We go two-by-two," he always told me.

I don't miss the worrying about his excessive behaviour, and the incredible highs and lows of living with someone so like me. But for the most part, he was a gentle soul who would have made a great dad. Once again cue in the "maybe, if only, should have, could have, would have". Fuck fuck fuck. When I close my eyes at night, I dance with him in my dreams, snuggling down under his armpit and inhaling his beautiful body smell, stroke his silky skin and feel him rest his chin on my head – me and my darling Steven together again.

I still think of him nearly every day ... when the sun sets and throws reds, yellows and pinks across the horizon, when owls hoot, in zany moments and during my crazy experiences, when I see pictures with slogans or funky signage, when I play raucously with my children and we scream with laughter, when I lie in bed lonely and sad.

Ken was my passionate first love, but Steven was my soul mate.

Chapter 16

Steven's death shattered me and I went through the motions of living in a trance. I was deeply in love with my son, adored my job and colleagues at *Fairlady* magazine, and was hooked on the electric energy of Johannesburg. But my life felt scarily disorientated.

Advice poured in: "Make no big decisions. Think before you act. Stay put for a while because Benjamin needs stability. You can't just get up and go. What about work?"

In retrospect, staying put was a very bad decision. I really needed to pick myself and baba up, and move back to Durban where I would have had support from my family and life would have slowed down.

I was heartbroken and incapable of bouncing back. I was paralysed with the anguished fatigue of grief and wasn't coping. I never had any food in the fridge – like NOTHING – and I drank too much, started smoking a few cigarettes every night and taking sleeping tablets to get to sleep. I was unable to work effectively or deal with any pressure at all. Workmates rallied around and tried to help me along but I was a helpless liability.

Steven had been such a significant helpmate and I'd been so pampered and cosseted in our nine years together, I struggled to care for myself. He'd cooked and shopped and sorted out the car and household maintenance. I didn't even know how to get the oven to work because, as I discovered, it wasn't as simple as pushing a button.

Then the malicious gossip started. Some started muttering about how I was cursed, that I had in some way caused Steven's and Ken's deaths. It seemed that being widowed once was understandable, but twice seemed too much of a coincidence. One spiteful photographer at work spread rumours that I was a wicked witch who had cast evil spells to kill Ken and Steven.

"He said you're a bad witch," a work colleague said. "Lots of us in the building are scared of you now."

I was so utterly crushed and devastated that I collapsed at work and was forced to take sick leave to deal with the horror of such accusations. How annoying that 11 years later this same photographer was begging the public for money for a hip operation, and my kind sister-in-law Bridget gave him one of Steven's pictures to auction to raise funds for his medical expenses. I am still surprised at how much his nastiness distresses and hurts me.

Attempts to take time out were never successful as there was always a picture editor phoning to ask about a photo, or a sub needing some extra information. I needed complete quiet in my head to sort out the chaos and should have turned off all contact with the world, and just been quietly alone with Benjamin. But I didn't. If only, I should have, I wish I had ...

I was tired all the time. I cried constantly – while I shopped, while walking my son in his pram, and during my gym session. Three months after the death of Steven, I went to an aggressive Afrikaans psychologist for help, but after two sessions, he was clearly annoyed with my victim mentality and told me to stop complaining and to be proactive.

However, once again, the universal power of the sisterhood kicked in and I made some lifelong friends, relative strangers sent by my guardian angels when I really needed them. Despite the sadness, I have bittersweet memories of wine, laughter and friendship. I was supported by some wonderful people who helped to pick me up and carry me along – including the editor of *Fairlady* at the time, Ann Donald, who arrived at my apartment with a bag of groceries and her gorgeous bestie, Shelagh, one very dark mental night. Ann intuitively realised I was teetering on the edge of despair, and took the time and trouble to intervene. And dear Shelagh became a shining light in those bleak days and we actually had many hilarious dinner parties and book club meetings in her gorgeously quirky home in the following months.

Another delight was meeting a wonderful friend, former journalist Maureen Isaacson, and we'd have copious cups of coffee at a coffee shop in Illovo while Ben ran amok, crumbling scones and spreading the cream and jam on the table and beyond. I hung out with my sister-in-law Bridget Hilton-Barber and Benjal's darling godfather, Andrew Meintjies, at weekends, and they would take my son off on Saturday mornings for baby adventures so I could easily catch up on chores. I have heart-warming memories of calmness at the home of the gentle photographer Giséle Wulfsohn. Both Andrew and Giséle have subsequently died in the last decade – Andrew was murdered and Giséle died from cancer – so I honour their memories here and think of them with gratefulness and love so very often.

I also kept in touch with other mums Steven and I had met at baby classes, including one whom I actually went on to share a room with at the Sandton Clinic when we gave birth to our sons. Since our babies were born on the same day, we held a joint first-birthday party at her massive Illovo home down the road from me. Unfortunately, her husband, a young investment broker, was horrified to have his home invaded by mums and bubs, mostly my friends as it turned out. He wanted us to hold the party in the driveway, but sadly it rained so we had to decamp to an outside veranda. The other mum-of-birthday-boy spent most of the party hiding upstairs, crying, because her husband was being so uptight and charmless. When everyone left, I bundled up Ben and fled home and ugly cried because I knew that if Steven had been alive, it would have been a party filled with incredible warmth, fun and laughter. With Steven, Ben's first birthday would have been an over-the-top celebration of silliness and frivolity. That day, 9 December 2002, I missed Steven with a deep and frightening pain.

So when Benjamin had a small testicular hernia and had to go to hospital for day surgery on 14 April 2003, I was really, really fragile. And so came about the very worst time of my entire life. Nothing prepared me for the next cruel twist life had in store for me.

Being widowed twice within the space of a decade means I've had to face death more than most. But nothing prepared me for the morning after his surgery when I walked into Benjamin's room to find my son dead.

Still sleepy and yawning, I wandered into Benjamin's room to pick him up for morning cuddles. As I reached down, a cold icy horror spread through my veins.

Lying face up, his eyes still open, his body was already still and blue, his face frozen like some kind of gargoyle.

All I could hear was the pounding of blood in my ears as my baby's blue face stared lifelessly from his cot. Then a deafening ringing vibrated in my head as a blanket of fog swept through my brain and seeped through my body. I couldn't think and the disbelief and horror paralysed me.

Dear merciful God, oh please, please let this be a nightmare … don't make this really be happening, I thought.

But it was tragically true. Due to confusion at the hospital dispensary with medication, he went into a coma after being given wrongly dispensed pain medication, and died all alone in his cot while I slept next door.

I stumbled around the apartment for a few minutes trying to get my head to kick into action. As I type this now, I feel my chest starting to thump and realise I still can't remember too much as my brain has mercifully blanked out big patches. But I phoned my dad.

"Benjamin is dead," I said.

"Are you sure?" he said.

"Yes," I replied.

"Monica, call the ambulance, call the ambulance right away," he said.

"It's no use," I said. "He's completely dead."

Then I phoned the surgeon at his home. His wife said the surgeon was in the shower and would call me back.

"My baby is dead," I said. "Help me."

The kind urologist was at my home in what seemed like minutes with neatly combed wet hair, immaculately dressed in a suit with his briefcase in hand, looking deeply distressed. But what could he do?

"Dear merciful God, please don't make me live through this," I kept saying. "Don't let this be happening to me."

The surgeon told me to go to the Sandton Clinic, then he spun smartly on his polished heels and left.

I didn't want to look at my dead son again. I couldn't look at him. He was just so very cold and frightening. Cotton wool endorphins filled every pore of my being and I floated along in a cloud of terror. The sun rose. I call Benjamin's godfather, Andrew Meintjies, who lived around the corner. White-faced and sweaty, Andrew ran up to the apartment wearing baggy grey tracksuit pants and a torn green T-shirt. Shaking and crying, he bundled him up in a duvet and we took him to Sandton hospital in his rusty VW jalopy. As we ran in with our pile of bedclothes and child, the staff looked bewildered and alarmed. They took Benjamin off. They ushered me off to another room where I begged and begged a passing doctor to simply euthanise me, to put me out of my misery like a dog. The pain was so intense, and the fear of living for even one second without Benjamin, and the memory of his death, was such agony, I was terrified. One had to peel me off him like a leech, and as more and more people arrived to support me and the family, so hospital staff became alarmed and swept us out into the car park. So we sat there, wondering what the hell to do, where to go, or how to proceed.

Sometimes people tell me that they can't imagine the pain of losing their child. I totally understand. All I can say is that if you do have a child, think of how you would feel if they suddenly died. Then multiply that level of pain many, many times. It is much worse that you can possibly imagine. Only mothers who have also lost a child understand the depth of that torture. To this day, I have no idea how we survive the death of our children. Perhaps we are so stunned, we don't have the brain power or energy to fling ourselves off the nearest building or gas ourselves in the car. But I do know if heartfelt wishes came true, I would be dead.

People flew in from across the world and different parts of the country for the funeral, and the immediate family camped out at the home of my brother, Andrew, and his wife Welma. My childhood friend Debbie arrived, bringing comfort from a time when our lives still stretched out blissfully before us, an unpainted landscape with futures only limited by our imaginations. She took time out to come with me to shop for a tracksuit and touch up the roots of my hair – in retrospect a weird thing to have done, but I couldn't think of what else to do and it was strangely comforting doing 'normal' girlie stuff.

A sister-in-law, Carol, simply lay down on the bed and wrapped me in her arms. A friend, Kate, gave me a book of her favourite poems. Another woman I didn't even know took the time to make me a beautiful and uplifting CD compilation of soothing music. I clung to the outpouring of love, heartbreak and genuine concern in cards and letters. One wonderful mum of a former colleague, Helen Grange, made us food. She hunted down my brother's address in Midrand, negotiated her way out there, then simply knocked and dropped. At a time when our family was just reeling with confusion, this was such a kind and thoughtful gesture. Others suggested I had been cursed and needed a sangoma to cleanse me, others took the opportunity to try to sell me their religion, and quite a few close friends couldn't cope and simply disappeared.

I popped back to my flat with my mum and sisters and packed up a suitcase of clothes; the last time I would ever enter that doomed flat again. I phoned a charity and told them to come and collect all Benjamin's stuff.

The funeral – held on Easter Saturday – was deathly quiet. The tiny white coffin was decorated with flowers and surrounded by photographs taken by Gisèle and Andrew. There was no music; the minister spoke only briefly. I insisted on no eulogy for my baby boy, just a most basic farewell to Benjamin's brief life. He'd been so central to the future of me, my family and the Hilton-Barbers, part of his beloved dad and a mini-Steven H-B who comforted us with his existence. Now even that had been cruelly ripped away.

I got through the first few days on tranquilisers and sleeping pills, carefully doled out by family, which was probably sensible at that time. And then I was put on a plane to Australia to stay with my sister Catherine who immigrated there a few years previously.

"Please let the plane crash," I begged so often my worried sister, already exhausted with the burden of my grief, snapped.

"Stop saying that," she said. "My daughters – your nieces – are waiting for us on the other side and they need me and I need them. All I want to do now is to hug them tight and never, ever let them go."

I stepped off that plane to face one of the most brutal journeys of survival. The next few months proved the most frightening period of my life, so dire my mind thankfully blanked much of it out. I have *no idea* how I endured such pain. So, there I was in Australia, now 40 years old, a double widow with a dead son.

As any of you who have experienced profound shock and anguish understand, my body responded by shutting down. I battled to recognise people or names, I struggled to do basic stuff and I became clumsy and stupid. But when that chemical waned and reality flashed, the intensity of the pain soon forced my brain to shut right back off again. To lose a beloved husband was heartbreaking and, both times, I felt all my hopes and dreams had been swept away, leaving me completely at a loss. So I concentrated all my time and energy on getting through each hour, then each day, until I could escape to sleep.

In comparison to losing a child, the death of a husband is like stubbing toes, but losing Benjamin took pain to a new level completely – up there with being stabbed in the chest repeatedly day in and day out.

Days spun by, life continued and I watched from the outside. Every cell in my body felt raw and enflamed, exhausted with the relentlessness of life. My tortured mind spun around and around and around, trying to work out how and why and what if, the fatigue making me crazy, and my overwhelming desire was to crawl under a rock and die. And every time a shard of clarity shone through the brain fog, anguish slammed into my stomach, leaving me breathless with agony.

Oh, the times I wanted to take my brain out and put it in the fridge to get some respite.

I was surviving in this sun-bleached country with its pleasant people and undemanding lifestyle. And despite the enormous concoction of opiate-type drugs that had naturally enveloped my mind in a detached fog of confusion, a basic animal instinct overwhelmed me ... to fall pregnant and have another child ... a reason.

Chapter 17

Australia is known as the Lucky Country, the enormous land of endless sunny days, wide open spaces and happy new immigrants.

I first visited Australia with Benjamin the Christmas after Steven's death. We came over to visit my sister, Catherine, who had moved to the Queensland Gold Coast with her two daughters and husband to escape South African crime a few years previously. That Christmas holiday, I was disparaging at how plain it all was: the sky and beaches bleached of any vibrant colour by the relentlessly hot sun, the fat, wishy-washy Sheilas and Bruces with their tattoos and missing teeth, the bland culture and sense of smug complacency, with so many working-class European and British immigrants. I was amazed how many South Africans had opted to leave South Africa with all the colourful energy and brilliant African culture – a country pulsating with promise and bristling with passionate intensity – for this sandy monument to mediocrity.

I had no idea that a few months later, I would be back again – this time alone, and at the lowest point of my life.

But when I arrived here after the death of Benjamin, I found it peaceful and welcoming, a soothing balm to my insane life of misfortune and madness. I appreciated the oceans with squeaky white sand and uninterrupted kilometres of shoreline, non-threatening shopping centres and a laid-back culture of "No worries, mate" and "Chillax, have a beer, put your feet up". Even drivers on the road were slow and polite, with most people following speed limits. Australia has horrendous fines for drunk driving, and certainly there were no noisy taxis mounting curbs, slamming on brakes and stopping anywhere, nor the endless cacophony of hooting and shouting.

I loved that the smorgasbord of well-maintained parks and nature areas had BBQ facilities with free gas and hot water, service was quick and efficient, and corruption was the exception rather than the norm. I adored the fact that neighbourhoods are fenceless, and going into the garden didn't make me nervous. Children rode their bikes to the park to meet their friends and hadn't ever heard the word 'apartheid'. Within days of living in Australia, I was leaving keys in the car, the house was unlocked, and I felt as safe as a rock in a cave.

I was in a beautiful country – but I was peering over the edge of hopeless despair. I was a wife with no husband, a mother without a child, a 40-year-old widow with nothing bar a truckload of traumatic baggage.

All I could think of was to fall pregnant again fast. So, within days of arriving, while hanging out with friends, I walked into a bar and saw this incredibly tall, rather aloof Aussie towering above the crowd.

From the moment I saw this man, I was smitten. Initially, I thought he was gorgeous, all long, lean and muscled with chiselled cheekbones.

I informed him straight up I wanted sex only for a baby. Despite his protests that he just wanted to take me sightseeing, I fed him heaps of tequila, gave him a blow job and he was good to go. The man hadn't had sex for half a year so he didn't stand a chance. He initially must have thought I was joking about the baby – until I sent him off to have his sperm tested when I didn't fall pregnant the first month. I wanted to check out his virility.

"Don't think you are getting all this sex for nothing," I kind-of joked. "If I am not pregnant soon, I am going to bill you."

My demands were so bizarre, it didn't for a second occur to

me it might be *me* – nearly 40 years old, not a month after the death of my child, in a new country, and in all sorts of extreme mental pain. I was still deeply in love with Steven and in the early, heart-bleeding stages of grieving for Benjamin, but I threw myself headlong into this new relationship because I was terrified of the massive, gaping black hole my life had become.

I spun his head out, threw his world upside down and rushed him off his feet. Before his brain had time to stabilise, we were married and I was pregnant. I clung to Husband Three, a lifebuoy in my turbulent sea of madness.

At first, Husband Three gave me a reason for living, a new country to call home, renewed hope and love. I was profoundly grateful and hugged him close, a beacon of promise and stability in my terrifying world of darkness and pain.

We married barefoot on Wategos Beach in Byron Bay, an hour from the Gold Coast – me in a long white dress and him in white linen pants and flowing white shirt. We had a handful of guests, mainly our families and my posse of new Aussie girlfriends. Our celebrant was an elderly woman we'd found in a newspaper and we took amateur pictures with small digital cameras. Afterwards, we picnicked in the shade until the rain closed in and we ran for shelter.

Our happiest days were in a tiny apartment on a main road close to the ocean in Palm Beach. We'd hang over the balcony, watching people in the service station across the road and listening in amusement to fights between the drug addicts, alcoholics and prostitutes, operating from the sleazy motel next door. His alarm would go off in the early morning and he'd be off to make kitchen bench tops in a factory, leaving me to roll into his warm, deliciously musky space to cuddle down. When he came home, we'd lie together on the couch, he'd feed me spoonfuls of ice cream while we listening to Xavier Rudd, Rodriguez, Philip Glass, trance, and melodic semi-classical music. We'd trade back massages, then, lying side by side in bed, read or watch sitcoms like *Frasier* reruns, *House* and *Doc Martin*. There was endless tenderness, kissing, stroking and caring.

When I cried, he comforted me, even though he couldn't

possibly understand, having never faced death or tragedy in his smooth-sailing and protected Australian life.

We told each other we were happy, that we loved each other. When he wrapped his arms around me and held me against his chest, for those few moments, I felt safe and protected and suitably adored. I have bittersweet memories of him giving me money "to buy yourself a present" when he got paid for a commission, of him buying me flowers when I felt down, us lying in bed after making love and feeling the cool breeze on our naked bodies while listening to the rustling of gum trees and the chattering of lorikeets.

Husband Three was a great distraction. But in that first year, I loved him as much as I possibly could, considering I had just lost my darling Steven and Benjal Bunny. I was certainly committed to our life together. And certainly, I believed that he loved me … Why else would a young guy choose to have a child and marry when nobody forced him to do either?

When music touched raw nerves one evening, I broke down and sobbed. He held me in his arms. When I felt tears falling from my forehead, I looked up and saw the tears falling onto my face were from him. He really felt my sorrow.

Being pregnant really helped. Despite endless advice by self-appointed experts not to fall pregnant again until I had accepted the death of Benjamin (ha ha – like I had decades to waste!), falling pregnant again was the best decision of my life. I had to keep mentally and physically healthy by nurturing myself. I tried to stay calm, and ate healthily and exercised gently.

At the time of my arrival in Australia, the news was filled with a murder case where three 20-something siblings had been murdered. When I saw television pictures of the sobbing mum, I felt so incredibly grateful to be me. It reminded me that no matter what my situation, at least I was young enough to have more children. I was so glad I wasn't that other mother.

Meanwhile, I was fortunate enough to be put in touch with two mothers who had also lost young children around the same time, also living on the Gold Coast, and if it wasn't for them, the pain might have been unbearable.

Kate lost her newborn daughter, Eloise, to SIDS and Fiona, already a mum of two sons, was struggling to deal with the death of her three-month-old daughter, Chloe.

One day, when Husband Three was away for work for a few days, I was seized with panic that I would not cope with the pain of my life. Later that day, I read an article in the local knock-and-drop newspaper highlighting Red Nose Day and discussing the work SIDS and Kids did with grieving parents. The journalist had interviewed Kate. So I phoned the SIDS and Kids Brisbane branch for support. The attendant SIDS and Kids counsellors made me tea and gave me hugs while I told them I had no idea how I was going to live with so much pain.

While I sobbed in their offices and flopped on their couch, the counsellors phoned Kate and Fiona, who jumped in a car and drove up from the Gold Coast to give me comfort, probably saving my life. They became my closest friends.

We formed our own club on the Gold Coast – The Dead Baby Society – where our motto was: "Life is Fucked and God is Not Our Friend." It was such a comfort and relief to be with others who knew how I felt. Fiona and Kate understood my frenzied chatter when I felt like I was going mad with grief, and in our darkest hours, we pulled each other through to the next day. At first, we railed against everyone and everything in the whole world, together we cursed the universe and hated all mothers, none of whom we thought deserved kids.

Yet we still managed to laugh about our irrational behaviour and confused fears, and shared emotions we would never have been able to discuss with 'ordinary' people. I teetered more than once on the cusp of insanity, and much of our humour was tinged with madness. We'd hash out all the details of our children's deaths in minutiae, inspecting it all closely, in case it hadn't really happened. And I would frequently have to pull over while driving, when a sobbing attack crashed over me, and phone them.

We met every few days. We phoned in between. We walked together on the beach and drank lots of coffee and ate cake after cake. We'd drive up to Brisbane and meet with other SIDS and Kids mums, and it consoled me to be among women who understood my pain. I felt 'normal', and I didn't feel alone. I will never forget the incredible kindness of the two social workers, Sonia and Dot, who cared for us all with such dedication, tenderness and love.

Our DBS (Dead Baby Society) increasingly found ourselves discussing plans for the future, sharing excitement about new projects and getting involved in living again. A year on, we might not mention death, grief or our lost little ones for entire conversations. But on sad anniversaries, we got together to eat more cake, drink wine and generally behave badly – with outings to theme parks and other venues with loads of adrenalin rushes when the going got tough. Sometimes we just went to the beach and screamed at seagulls.

Within two years, Kate, Fiona and I went on to have seven children between us. Kate had Lucinda, then I had Yannik nine months later. Eight months after Yannik's birth, Kate had Matthew and seven months on, I had Soren. Fiona, after two miscarriages during this time, fell pregnant with triplets while I was pregnant with Soren. At first we teased her about it, saying it might have been a case of being careful what you wish for. When she gathered Kate and me around to tell us, I joked and said: "This is proof that God really *does* hate you." Touchingly, Fiona called one of her triplets Benjamin, and Kate's son was born on Benjamin's birthday – 9 December. And these children could not be more loved and treasured by their mums, who remain so very, very grateful we have them all in our lives.

For the first year, I wrapped myself in Husband Three and the Dead Baby Society, put my head down and waited for time to pour soothing oils on the emotional havoc in my heart. Of all the times in my life, my survival instinct told me this was not a time to give in to self-indulgent dramatics. Any wobble might prove lethal, so I dug in and built my nest of self-created family stability out of anyone and anything I could stretch out and grab onto.

Chapter 18

Marriage Three didn't turn out the way I expected.

Despite my instant attraction and reckless bonding to Husband Three, just months into our marriage I had moments of fantasising about divorcing him.

"You are not who I need you to be. I don't respect you. I don't even like you. If I see you mutilating any more blocks of stone with power tools and calling it art, I will scream. I just wish I could erase you completely out of my life," I would mutter to myself.

Everything was set up for this relationship to fail, but all my hopes were pinned on it. I simply wanted to be married to the father of my children where we'd live in a little house, maybe get a dog, and have enough money to travel abroad once a year. I was done with excitement and over adventure. I craved to love and be loved. Despite my unfortunate history, I fantasised that perhaps it was going to be possible for my dream of my own family to finally come true.

But first off, the chances of me picking wisely were not good. I came with baggage, mega fucking baggage, and was in *no fit state* to be choosing husband number three. I picked him out with an unlucky Pooh finger. However, as I've said in earlier chapters, getting married and having a child was the only way I could think of to survive.

The foundations of our marriage were sandy and Husband Three was unable to emotionally or financially support even himself with any confidence. Whenever he hurt me, I would escape into a daydream where he didn't exist.

Cracks in our marriage slowly eroded into crevices. Dangerous signs were there right from the start, even in the initial honeymoon phase.

"The first time we met, I thought you were too loud, too attention-seeking," he told me. "I couldn't stand you."

I, on the other hand, was initially enamoured. However, I didn't take proper note of the small, close-set, cold eyes. I mistook his quietness for calm, his smirk for a smile, and failed to see his many insecurities blanketed under the cheap veneer of arrogance. But the truth is, compared to me at that stage, he appeared to have it all tightly under control.

I've certainly never found out what his motivation was to be with me, why he agreed to have our son Yannik, or why he stayed with me any time at all. Perhaps he was swept up in my whirlpool and was too weak to swim out. I presume he was swept away by the tragic pathos of my life, and having only been exposed to the typically bland Aussie life, was rather bowled over by this much-older woman with such a tragic past and overwhelming personality, which smacked him in the face like a tornado. The exhilaration and euphoria of initial attraction caused him to behave recklessly, probably for the only time in his life.

Whatever – it's just one of the many things about our marriage I have to accept not understanding.

I didn't take notice of details warning that ours was an ill-fated match. I ignored the fact that we couldn't enjoy romantic walks on the beach because I like to walk briskly and he likes to slowly saunter – really, really slowly, so slowly I could hardly contain my rising hysterical frustration. It didn't occur to me that the nine years' difference in age would pose a problem. Perhaps it didn't, but his relative youth often made me feel truly embarrassed and awkward in public, and I was always waiting for our marriage to fail.

He is organised and systematic and dislikes impulse whereas I am all about slapdash spontaneity, careless bohemia and higgledy-piggledy patterns. When we met, his way to unwind was to smoke marijuana at the weekend, although to his credit, he stopped smoking weed because, for me, that would have been a deal breaker at that point in my life. But he refused to give up his LSD-fuelled trance parties in the bush. I abhor both trance and acid. He enjoys eating out and drinking wine. Fine dining and drinking alcohol bore me immensely.

Then there was the incident with the cheese slicer. I accidentally broke his well-used silver cheese slicer quite soon after we met. The handle and cutter parted ways while I was using it, and he was really disproportionately uptight about it. He made me pay $120 (R1 300) to have it soldered back together again.

Initially, I told myself our differences were good, that opposites attract, and we could meet somewhere in the middle. Of course, we had some things in common, like reading, movies, art and fear of being trapped in large, crowded places. But even then, he preferred action and sci-fi while I like documentaries and drama.

Right from the start, basic fundamental needs were not being met. He needed to be admired and respected, and wanted a strong-minded and sensible woman to care for him financially and in every other way, putting him first above all other. I wanted a strong-minded and passionate person to put family and me first at all times; a rock-solid provider to lean on, like Ken, or wrapped up in the warm and adventurous personality of Steven. Husband Three offered neither.

The first flush of romance quickly faded and disappointment set in on both sides.

Instead of being treated like a princess during pregnancy, I was told daily: "This is what women are born to do – and it's what you wanted – so quit complaining."

My pregnancy with Yannik was very different to my pregnancy with Benjamin. This time I was all alone at my scans, single in my decisions, without any respect or sympathy from the father of my child.

"This is what you wanted," he kept saying. "This is what women are born to do."

The tension between us as Yannik's birth approached was so stressful. On the day I was to have the child, I accidentally bumped his car reversing out. He was apoplectic with rage.

It wasn't easy, as I was reminded that I missed both Steven and Benjamin terribly as I went through each stage of the pregnancy. A baby fathered by another man was taking up space where Benjamin once lived. The combination of grief and hormones was exhausting. I was perpetually anxious something would go wrong and went for scans weekly to ensure the unborn baby was still alive.

He was born by Caesarean at 37 weeks on 5 April 2014, 10 days before the first anniversary of Benjamin's death. I had Yannik a few days earlier than planned because, with the upcoming anniversary and Husband Three's tension, I panicked and insisted the doctor operate on the Monday rather than the Wednesday as scheduled. But his little lungs were not quite ready so he started life in an incubator with a drip in his arm. Morphined out of my head, I sat next to the glass box looking at his chest rising and falling, crying. Husband Three and my family made it clear that my hysterical demands to have the baby two days early was yet another sign that I was an unstable and irresponsible mother. Then, because of the distress, I couldn't produce enough milk, so Yannik struggled and refused to breastfeed.

Initially, my little Yannie Bunny was high maintenance as he cried a lot and slept little. I was uptight so he was unsettled and overstimulated. His little hands would fly around and he'd whack himself in the face. After six weeks of little sleep, I took him to a nursing sister who taught me how to bundle him and make him secure. From that day, he became Pure Angelic Perfection.

My darling Yan Bun was proof that perhaps God was there looking out for me. He was a perfect, beautiful treasure. I grew a new heart just for Yannik and he gave me every reason to survive and made my life worthwhile and happy again.

Motherhood was bliss and my mummy heart was filled with

incredible happiness. But, on the marriage front, all was not well between husband and wife. When our baby arrived, Husband Three made Yannik and me sleep on a tiny couch in the living room so his sleep wasn't disturbed. When Yannik was a few weeks old, Husband Three then took himself off on an overseas trip to visit his Dutch aunties. On his return, Husband Three, Yannik (two months old) and I went to a wedding on a neighbouring island. A glass or two of wine on many weeks of no sleep meant I fell asleep at the table. Husband Three was so furious he'd been left holding the baby that he was set to take the last ferry back, leaving me fast asleep and alone on the island overnight. Fortunately, a woman at the wedding noticed and rescued me. Husband Three stomped about, red-faced with rage, for weeks after.

"It was my friends, so I should have been free to party – you should have bloody stayed home," he said.

I desperately wanted another child. Husband Three was fiercely against this as he believed he had only signed up for one.

"But in my wedding vows, I talked about children," I cried.

But two seemed too much for him to handle. So it was up to me.

Three months after Yannik was born, I stopped breastfeeding so Husband Three hauled me off to the doctor for a Depo Provera contraceptive injection.

"I'm not that bloody stupid," he claimed. "You can't trick me with lies about taking the pill."

When the doctor called my name out to go into his room, Husband Three wanted to come in with me. Fortunately for me, the doctor prevented him actually coming into the consulting room.

"Doctor, I am really run down, perhaps I should just have a vitamin B injection," I said.

When I got home, Husband Three asked to see my injection mark.

"See, all fixed," I said.

The following month I was pregnant.

Husband Three was justifiably furious. He called it my Help-Yourself Baby. My birthday is the day before Christmas and that year I got a combined present – a dust buster. Yip, you read that right – a dust buster. I cried. I pleaded. I ate humble pie. I apologised and tried to explain that this new little life was Meant To Be and A Precious Gift – and he would of course love it. He said that was not the point, that I had disrespected him, nullified his right to choose, and that he could never trust me again. I reckon the ends justified the means. To see them together now – where he loves our perfect second child so utterly and completely – it's hard to see why Husband Three can't accept that ultimately, it was worth a little deception.

But Husband Three was unforgiving. After that Christmas, he took off to Sydney, planning not to return to me. I made plans to take Yannik and my pregnant self and move out of state. Then his father died unexpectedly, and he had to come home. So, with no time or energy to divorce, we continued our marriage. For this pregnancy, I was entirely on my own physically and emotionally. No sex. No real conversation. No love. Not even hugs. To show how sorry I was to have been forced to trick him, I let him choose our baby's name. I agreed this would be the last baby, and that I'd tie my tubes after he was born. How much more could I do, for goodness sake? But he had started to dislike me.

"You don't respect me and I don't trust you," he would say over and over again, like a broken record.

Despite the growing marital unease, the day Soren was born was one of the happiest of my life. When Soren was born, I had none of the depression and postnatal distress I experienced with Yannik. I knew what to expect. I was relaxed and so excited to see him. When I saw his chubby face with the dimple in the chin, I fell completely and totally in love. I stroked his fingers, his silky hands, his crumpled toes, his mottled pink legs and his round tummy. I was so enchanted with him, I couldn't sleep for a week. I just sat up gazing adoringly at him. Husband Three was very late fetching me the day I was discharged, as he had taken time to cook himself a leisurely breakfast at home, even though I told him the hospital had turned me out of my room for another patient. I had to wait in the corridor.

As I walked in the door at home, Yannik jumped into his baby chair and pulled his brother onto his lap for a cuddle – and it was the start of their incredibly close relationship. I just wanted to gather my babies into my arms and love them all day and night. My life became a blur of nappies, bottles, picnics and parks, early nights, mothers' clubs, baby faces snuffling into my neck, tiny hands around my neck, soft cuddles, children's stories and the Wiggles. The next five years, wrapped in the pink love bubble of motherhood, I floated on this amazing baby high and, despite the disappointment of my failing marriage, I was remarkably content.

Husband Three struggled with fatherhood. He wanted me to spend time with him alone, to be a wife and not a mum all day every day.

"You always put the kids before me," he said. "I am always last in your life."

So Grumpy Pants stayed well away quite a bit, even on weekends. He determinedly stuck to his 'you're on your own' philosophy. So much so that when I sliced the tops of my fingers on a sharp steel rod on the outside wash line, he wouldn't help me. Soren was just three weeks old and I was carrying him in a baby papoose while Yannik pottered next to me. I was trying to hang the washing but the line needed to be hooked back onto a steel rail. I slipped and accidently hung onto an exposed steel plate, which sliced the tops off the four fingers on my left hand. Blood was pumping out all over Soren, onto Yannik's little white-haired head, and dripping onto the grass. I staggered inside and phoned Husband Three to come home and help.

His reply? "I hope you didn't break the wash line."

"I can't come now," he continued. "It's your problem, you deal with it," he said, followed by his favourite rallying cry: "After all, having kids is what you wanted."

His rant finally ended with: "And don't think that I am going to be helping you with nappy changes – you sort it out."

I phoned my sister, who raced over and drove me to my doctor and cared for the kids while I got four fingers stitched back together.

It was a roller-coaster ride. One minute, I felt ultra-tense with Husband Three and I wanted to run. The next, I looked at my beautiful family and my heart was so full of love and pride and contentment. And my Australian journey seemed so sunny and bright, and I felt so grateful to be living in this paradise.

But the road to the Land Down Under wasn't smooth. I had arrived on a tourist visa. However, once I had fallen pregnant and emotionally connected to Husband Three, I didn't want to go home. So I began the long process of getting my visa changed to a temporary visa, then onto a permanent visa and then, hallelujah, the ultimate immigrant's prize – Australian citizenship.

I went to the ceremony alone as my kids were at school and Husband Three and I were already drifting apart, so he didn't bother. Instead, a work colleague came along unexpectedly – another blessing from the Universal Sisterhood – and I felt quite teary and proud to sing the Aussie national anthem while waving the flag. I then gobbled a few meat pies with tomato sauce, scoffed a vegemite sarmie before picking up a potted baby gum tree, and heading home.

Within two weeks, my sons and I all had Aussie passports. Aussie Aussie Aussie. Oi Oi Oi.

But changing nationalities isn't like changing a pair of dirty panties. I left behind Monica the Journalist and Wife of Two Well-Loved Photographers to marry Mr Boring Nobody where I became a housewife, part-time down-table sub on a local knock-and-drop and mother of two small children. Nobody knew I was Fabulous or Interesting. To them, I was just a middle-aged Aussie immigrant. Most colleagues and acquaintances knew nothing beyond that I was South African-born with Aussie family. With so few knowing about past husbands and Benjamin, I sometimes felt quite discombobulated and often lonely.

One day, when the kids started to pull out of early babyhood into toddlerdom, I woke up next to a long-limbed, curly-haired young man and thought to myself:

"Fuck, who the hell are you? Where's Steven? What am I doing here? Whose suburban life is this I've landed in?"

"EEEEEK!"

Then I turned over to see the gorgeous little boys tucked into my side of the bed, tussled blond heads sharing my pillow, limbs flung carelessly across me and their kissy lips snuffling contentedly. My heart somersaulted and tears welled up. "AHHHHHH ... my okka Aussie sons."

I've never been so happy as when home with my sons. But when I felt that Husband Three was putting me down, divorce was this beautiful place I promised to visit when I had a bit of time, energy and money. When he walked round the house judging my housework, when he turned his nose up at my dinner and mocked my parenting, divorce was the calm place I went to when I gave up hope for us. It was a space where I could make my own decisions, control the parenting and finances, get a dog, foster children, move cities, move countries, teach abroad, or take a year-long road trip with my sons.

I used to joke about only marrying him for the kids and the Australian passport, and once I had both, his work would have been done. And yes, in the last few years of our marriage, divorce seemed to have a lot to recommend it. But when our marriage finally limped to an end, I was utterly and completely devastated.

*Monica and Ken Oosterbroek, 1991 (*The Star*)*

Thokoza, picture by Ken Oosterbroek

Monica and Ken, Lost City, Sun City, 1994

*Ken and Monica,
Namibian
Independence
concert, 1991
(Kevin Carter)*

Monica and Ken, 1992

Monica and Ken on their wedding day, 1991 (Karen Sandison)

Israel, 1991 (Ken Oosterbroek)

Ken and Monica at the Grand Canyon, 1992

Skiing in Colarado, 1992

*Eastern
Transvaal, 1992
(Ken Oosterbroek)*

Steve and Monica, Uganda, 1995 (Robin Comley)

Steve and Monica, Kingswalden, 1994

*Steve and Monica
bungee jumping, 1995*

Steve and Monica at Badlands America, 1995

Steven and Monica in Fulham Magistrate's court with the Mansfield sisters, 1994

Steven and their pets, Wilwee and Sir Edward Montgomery, an excellent and outstanding bear

Wedding pictures of Steven and Monica in a photo booth in Covent Garden, London, 1994

Nelspruit, 1995

Steven and Benjamin, Johannesburg, December 2001

Boys and Monica at carol service, 2007

Monica and the boys, Gold Coast, 2007

Boys and Monica near Cloncurry in the Outback, 2012

*Benjamin Nicolson
Hilton-Barber*

*Benjamin and Monica, 2002
(Gisele Wulfsohn)*

Monica with Yannik and Soren, 2012

Monica and her boys, Gold Coast Miami Beach, 2011 (Rick Morton)

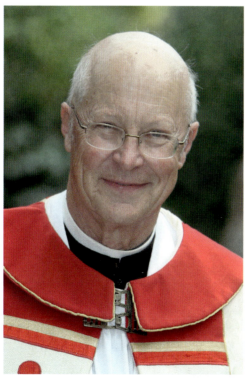

Monica's dad the Rev. Dr Ronald Nicolson

Monica and boys,
Stanthorpe, 2006

Monica with her mother, Howick, 2009

Megan East, Mike Downey, April Lynd, Kimbra Hicks, Monica Zwolsman and Jonene Richards, Gold Coast

Monica, Lucy and Catherine

Kate Chipman, Fiona Irvine and Monica Zwolsman

Monica, Yannik and Soren, Gold Coast, 2014 (Presto Photographies)

Chapter 19

Marriage to Husband Three might not have been going along so smoothly but the first six years in Australia contain some of the happiest moments of my life.

The stand-out highlight of my existence has been raising my children. I love being a mother with every cell in my body. With the wisdom of hindsight, if I had to live my life again, I would find a loving man who was a good provider, and settle down in Australian suburbia to have at least five children, dedicating my whole self to raising them. Being a mum has been the most extraordinary and rewarding experience in every possible way, and the ultimate purpose of my life. Children really are, for me, a miracle. Bearing and birthing a child is a fundamental religious experience and proof that God really does exist. And I have treasured every stage of being a mum so far.

Recently, I was talking to an old South African school friend I hadn't seen for three decades or more. We met up in a leafy park next to a beach and my sons were kicking a soccer ball around next to us.

"Your life has been so incredibly sad," she said. "I hoped you would find happiness at last, here in Australia. But now it turns out Husband Three made you miserable."

And, as I watched my boys running about with their white-blond hair flopping in the breeze and their startling blue eyes filled with mischief and life, I realised that my time in Australia, despite the marriage, has actually been filled with incredible and perfect joy.

"Are you kidding me?" I replied. "These have been the best days of my life."

It's true. Every day when I look at my sons, I am blissed out. My marriage might have been tense for at least half that time, but I barely noticed because I was so wrapped up in the pink candyfloss haze of mummydom.

All my children I planned for, like a military operation. Benjamin's short life taught me the sharpness of regret, and I was determined that this time round I would make every effort to be true to my idea of how to raise my new sons. I made myself available to them as much as possible so I wouldn't miss any precious moments.

I gave up being a journalist when my boys started kindergarten so I could fetch them at lunchtime every day. But it wasn't a sacrifice. When I arrived in Australia, I worked two days a week as a down-table sub to fit my lifestyle to pregnancy and early childhood. Fortunately, an upside of my marriage was the kindness and generosity of Husband Three's Dutch mum who not only looked after my boys on the two days I worked, but also cleaned the house and left us cooked meals. After working in Africa, with the birth of democracy in South Africa and my raft of wild travel and adventure stories, Australian news felt bland. In May 2008 my local paper devoted an entire front page to a popular rugby player who had not been selected to play for the state of Queensland in an inter-state competition. The following day, the front page was filled with his wife's reaction to his exclusion. This was despite a massive earthquake in China where 70 000 people died and five million had been left homeless.

"If I work on this paper long enough, will I too think rugby is the most worthy front-page news?" I wondered.

So I retrained. I did a postgrad diploma in Education, completed a TESOL (Teaching English as a Second Language) course and started my new career at the age of 45, teaching.

Today, I teach English to foreign students from around the world – mainly Asia, South America and Europe. Most of them are in their early twenties, taking a gap year after completing degrees and starting their careers. I love their enthusiasm and energy. The dynamic multicultural interaction placates my adventurous heart, the four-hour working day fits perfectly with motherhood duties, and caring for all my students appeals to my indefatigable mothering instinct.

Sometimes people say stupid shite like: "Well, when your sons get to be teenagers, you can get your life back and work full-time again."

But I can't imagine a situation so dire I would be forced to leave two hormone-crazed boys home alone every afternoon and during the holidays! Ha. I imagine they'd be smoking bongs, fighting off the amorous advances of skanky ho's and getting up to god-knows what if I won't be there to monitor the home front.

So my balance here in Australia between work and motherhood is perfect, and I do feel very blessed and grateful to have this option.

Looking back at video footage and pictures, it's clear that I was the primary parent, with Husband Three often away – either working or holidaying without us. He wasn't keen on pooping, whingeing babies or toddlers and said changing nappies made him vomit.

As a mum of two little ones under the age of two, my days were spent on the Gold Coast beaches and in the leafy parks with other mums. The routine included getting outdoors early, spreading out blankets in the shade for kids, packing up loads of tea and cake for the mums, and we'd loll about laughing and gossiping until lunchtime. Then it was home for an afternoon nap followed by toddler music or swimming or a dancing lesson in the afternoon.

It was such a gentle, friendly time. On some Sundays, Husband Three and I would explore with kids in tow. We'd hike with the kids in backpacks, cycle with the boys in their baby seats in the back, or stop at a neighbourhood park where our sons would run, slide, whirl and swing. There were endless games of chase and tickle, Bear Hunting and re-enactions of *The Three Little Pigs*.

These were the best times in our marriage and I treasure those precious memories.

Shopping was always a giggle as both boys refused to wear clothes at all until they were at least three years old, and would often head out nudie. Or they would insist on fluffy pink Barbie shoes with wand and matching plastic handbag, hand-me-downs from girl cousins, usually filled with marbles and Lego pieces. Knowing lollies and chocolates were an absolute no-no (I'm militantly anti-junk food for my children), they'd grab a bar of chocolate at the checkout aisle, take a big bite, and then run and hide. I'd have to crawl under displays and shelving in pursuit to drag them out from some dusty corner.

I have experienced a childhood exploring worlds I barely knew existed because of my sons. Instead of tea parties and fairies, I've learnt about dinosaurs and dragons, diggers and rocks, planes and boats, martial arts and weaponry.

When they were pre-schoolers, we'd rush out to inspect every motorised sound – be it in the air or on the road – and not a helicopter or plane passed our house unnoticed, with both of them outside, pointing up, with much excitement. On Friday – garbage truck day – both boys raced up the driveway to experience the mechanical magic of the steel arm coming out and lifting up the bin and tipping rubbish in. The garbage man knew us so well, he'd stop by for tea. I've been to science exhibitions, I can build a guinea-pig cage, and I know all the rules to cricket, soccer and touch rugby.

My overriding joy is that both my boys are very loving and affectionate. From a young age until now, they regularly bowl me over with running hugs and boisterous attacks of love, often bruising my cheekbones and nose with enthusiastic dive-in kisses. When Yannik was two years old, he told me he "lubbed" me for the first time. He presented me with a flower (well, actually a weed) and I was so touched, I cried. Actually, I cried a lot in the early days of their childhood, tears of joy, because they were just so incredibly sweet and cute and my heart was so full of love, it hurt.

When the new animated movie *Happy Feet* came out, Soren

waddled around like a penguin for weeks. He'd always be holding a handful of toys, including Po'Bear (Polar Bear), Dog-Dog and Hippo (actually Eeyore) and a sackful of di-dors (dinosaurs). Di-dors were a big hit in our house and my sons liked nothing more than hunting them down. They were convinced all boulders and rocks were dinosaur eggs and, on one occasion, they sat down to wait for one to hatch. They were both thoroughly satisfied when a monstrous monitor lizard scuttled down a tree and out from behind a rock – clearly a small dinosaur hatched from a nearby stone.

We initially sent Yannik to a Catholic school and he was intrigued by Jesus and the Cross story. When we went camping during the Easter vacation, the boys would walk with me on the beach and chat to early-morning fishermen. Yannik kept asking people, "Did you know Jesus died on the cross for your sins?" Meanwhile, Soren, now obsessed with genitalia, said "Check out my willie. Check out how big it can grow. Look, I can push it in and out." It was during this stage taking him to any public toilets was hazardous. He'd slip under the doors and pop up to surprise whoever was in there, where he would discuss their 'panny'. He was also very keen on telling people he was not bought in a shop, that his mum and dad 'made' him.

"But is very dark inside Mummy's tummy because she didn't put the light on," he'd say.

Yannik just wanted to know what part of him I made and what his dad made.

"Did you make my legs, Mum, or did Dad? Who made my arms?"

Once they grew older, Christmas became really fun. The first Christmas they were old enough to understand, I spent time teaching them traditional carols, like "Away in a Manger" and "Hark the Herald Angels Sing". Yannik was intrigued by the Angel of the Lord who was going to announce: "Fear not, for I bring you good tidings."

When the boys were pre-schoolers, they spent one Christmas eagerly awaiting the Angel of the Lord. With sheets wrapped round them and tied with rope, belts and ribbon, they sat at the front door for the Angel to arrive in a bright white light at our door to tell us Jesus had been born. Then they planned to follow a bright, bright star to Bethlehem. For the journey, Soren was armed with a pair of chopsticks to stab the eyes of anyone who tried to steal his money (some confusion here about collecting taxes and stealing money!). For emergencies along the route, he had a few handfuls of 5c pieces in his undies (I always put $20 in my bra when we are out and about but he, of course, had neither bra nor a $20 note so he settled for what he had!). And, according to his logic, if anyone stole his money, they would be arrested because "people can't touch my privates, can they, Mummy?" This meant much jingling about, then me peeling 5c pieces off his sticky hot little nether regions once he was asleep. When the Angel didn't arrive, they showed absolutely no interest in the Christmas story again. I tried to convert them to the magic of Santa Claus, but both boys pronounced Santa was "disgusting". Yan told me that Santa was "fat", and therefore "a bad man".

As babies, the boys were inseparable. Soren followed "Yan-Yan" everywhere and mimicked his every move. At kindergarten, they spent playtime holding hands between the fences separating class playgrounds, until it was so difficult, staff would put them together. When Soren was in trouble at kindergarten, he would scream for his big brother who would be furious with teachers for making his brother cry. Even if I told off one, the other rushed to defend, telling me not to be horrible "to my bruda" and they would state they were "a little cross" with me and ordered me to time out "right now".

And we often had dramas. Soren fell into a lake while trying to look at ducks. I had to dive in to rescue him, cutting open a leg, losing shoes and ruining my mobile phone in the process. Soren survived with only a chomped lip but sweet Yannik, who wailed with fear, suffer from post-traumatic stress for weeks. While Yan and I shook and cried, Soren was delighted to be centre stage, waving and blowing kisses to the gathered crowd like he was royalty when I carried him back to the car.

As they got older, our conversations grew funnier. Their excuses were hilarious. When Soren was four years old, I walked into his room to find his curtain rail, curtains and huge patches of wall lying on the floor. When asked what happened, he replied: "I was just sitting quietly on my bed, saying a prayer to God, when it all fell down."

This, from a child who likes to preface every accident report with "I was on my way to give you a kiss when ..."

I was reading this pirate adventure with saucily named pirate One-Eyed Willy (presumably named to amuse parents as such boyish humour goes over the heads of little ones still). Attempts to get to the treasure are foiled by numerous booby traps. Later, Soren picks up my bra off the bed and hands it to me saying: "Here, Mum, don't forget your booby trap!" The whole time he was imagining One-Eyed Willy being tripped up round every corner by women's lingerie.

Soren did not cope when Yan started school without him. Soren cried, threw tantrums, and lost all his baby fat in his baby depression. They began to share a bed and I would find them in the mornings, cuddled up together. Of course, the moment Husband Three was away the boys were right into my bed armed with an array of blankies and soft toys. Even today, I find myself sharing my bed with sons and a menagerie of woolly animals.

Their wonder at life is inspiring. Like so many little people, they are intrigued with the infinity of the universe, that stars shining down on us could have been dead for millions of years, life after death, the spirit world and ghosts. The possibilities are only limited by their imaginations.

The funniest conversation was when Yan and Soz started learning about children being born. Last year, they asked me how they got out of my tummy. I showed them my C-section scar.

"Oh, thank goodness," said Yannik. "A boy in my class said he came out his mum's vagina!"

I explained that yes, that *did* happen to some babies.

"Daddy came out of Nanna's vagina," I told him.

Both boys were falling about with childish horror.

"Mum!" Yan said. "That's disgusting. That's not true, is it?"

But not as horrible as Soren who, when just three years old and enjoying nappy-free time during a picnic with a friend, climbed in her car and pooped in her basket. Soren's comment when I tried to discuss the error of his way?

"Pardon me," he said, his little head hanging down to one side trying out his remorseful look.

I pride myself on the fact that my kids are creative and adventurous both in thought and deed. Soren sometimes can't go to class because of something that makes his heart "too heavy for his legs to carry". They climb up everything and sometimes refuse to come down. We got kicked out of Chinese classes because Soren kept escaping; Nippers (lifesaving teams for kids) told us never to return and one school's (a Catholic one) parents actually held a petition to get us to leave. I think this was because my child explained that Jesus was not the son of God, and then wrestled a boy to the ground when the boy told him otherwise. To the school's credit, they were very understanding but since no parent would allow their kids to play with mine after that, we moved to another school.

Our adventures have been epic. The boys and I travelled round Australia in our camper van and visited South Africa a few times, but our weekend travels have been most consistent and exciting. It was always just us three – Husband Three never cared to join us, and when he did it wasn't nearly as much fun. But sometimes it was lonely being the only one responsible for two boys. One weekend on the Noosa coast, an hour out of Brisbane in Australia, I was watching my elder son, then about five years old, frolicking in the waves. As his confidence grew, he jumped further and further into the sea. I was consumed with flashes of terror as I imagined a tsunami sweeping him out to sea while I watched helplessly from the beach with Soren on my hip. I longed to be a 'real' family with their dad to help.

Later, Soren disappeared while I was putting shoes on Yannik.

"Have evil people stolen him, Mummy?" Yannik said, while I started shouting for Soren, heart thumping wildly. Soren was just a few metres along the beach, being loved and adored by a group of young teenage girls.

Then we hit a cyclone. Returning home that evening, the sun was shining behind us but we were driving into a green bank of clouds. When the rain hit, it was so heavy I couldn't see 10 metres, and car lights vanished in front of me. The roar of the wind, and the thundering sound of rain on our car, made it difficult to be heard. I had to blindly pull over, turn on my hazards and watch in horror as the deafening rain intensified, looking at trees pulled horizontal by the ferocious wind. Our camper trailer was whipped round at a 90-degree angle. The whimpering from the backseat became screams of panic, and I climbed into the backseat and pulled both boys into my lap, feeling the car lifted and rocked by the gale force. I sang songs and told jokes. But when we got home and the kids were safe inside I phoned my sister, Catherine, and burst into tears.

I'm tougher now and my kids are bigger. In fact, they save me these days. On a recent camping trip, I fell down a cliff one night while trying to build a fire too close to the edge. It was my eight-year-old son who bravely navigated his way to the bottom, pulled me out a river bed, and helped me climb back to safety.

Discipline is not really my thing. I tend to let the children run wild. I like to negotiate with them. However, when the kids were smaller, I nicknamed their father 'Major Dad' because he believed you can't and shouldn't reason with a child. His favourite saying was "You boys don't have to like me but you will bloody well respect me". So when Husband Three was away, the boys and I would eat peanut butter from the jar with our fingers, ride bikes through the house, picnic in bed and play hide-and-seek at bed time. And when Husband Three returned home, the kids and I flew about tidying. Unfortunately, when Husband Three tried to discipline the kids, they would run and hide behind me, making it very difficult for him to bond with the boys.

My marriage was crumbling around me but I only cared about my children. Anyone and everything else faded into the distance as I focused all my love and attention on raising my sons with a single-minded concentration – with great enthusiasm and full-on energetic application. It was exhausting and I had no time or energy left to spare.

Chapter 20

I didn't just wake up one day and think: "Okay, this is it, I am outta here." For me, it was a bewildering process. I needed proof that it was really, truly and completely over. I kept waiting for something that made it impossible NOT to leave. I wanted closure, a flashing neon sign that our marriage was killed, dead forever, that opting out was beyond doubt the only option left. So I waffled and faffed about, wasting years in this grey fog of marital depression and discontent. I wanted the decision to leave to be clear-cut and easy. But, as any divorcee will tell you, for most of us, it never really is.

I was unable to gently extricate myself from this ill-fitted marriage. I couldn't give up because I feared that the agony of divorce would drag me over the edge into a deadly abyss of despair. I got caught in a downward whirl of negativity, scared stiff by the thought of leaving.

We spent our marriage teetering on the brink of divorce. After Soren, our next real crunch was a year later, when Husband Three went to a symposium and, I felt, made no effort to phone me regularly or visit despite working close enough to commute daily. I was so hurt and angry, I put the house on the market. I seriously planned to leave. In retrospect, I really should have.

Instead, we decided to buy a bigger, better house, to upgrade and start a new life together in a fabulous tree house in the Gold Coast hinterland. It should have been paradise as it was surrounded by nature, possums, koalas, wallabies in the back yard, and lots of space.

But it felt all wrong. I felt imprisoned by trees. It was dark because the hills killed the sun early. The timber house required constant work to maintain. Instead of being restful, it soon felt too far from friends and the gym, making it impractical to pop out for a quick visit or workout. Then Husband Three bought a factory, taking $100 000 from his mother (earmarked for her retirement) and I felt that this put us under financial pressure.

Furthermore, Yannik developed a serious tree allergy so was constantly sneezing and rubbing his red, swollen eyes. And the house looked so romantic but the layout didn't encourage family unity. Husband Three spent too much time downstairs in the office, which was difficult to access at night as it involved flights of slippery and steep stairs outside, and running the gamut of possums. So I stayed upstairs with the kids and he stayed down.

I left him for six weeks and went to South Africa. He reluctantly joined us for a few weeks, and my impression was that he hated both me and the country. He was profoundly discontent and miserable, and I was resentful and, though I tried, he was impenetrable in his stony disapproval of me and where I came from. On our return, he suggested we part. By the next day, 25 February 2012, I had organised a townhouse back in the city of Gold Coast, and was packed and ready to go.

We moved into a complex with a swimming pool and tennis court, so it initially felt like a holiday resort. But soon living close to so many families and children was claustrophobic after our 11-hectare plot in the middle of a forest. Husband Three stayed the first night with us. Then the kids and I spent a few nights back at our tree house. The next week, Husband Three went off to a trance party and I told the kids their dad and I had separated. Yan knew all about divorce from school, and that in Australia, a year after separation, couples could divorce.

"Please, Mummy, don't do this to me," he begged. "Is it me and Soren?"

159

I gave him the story about his dad needing a bit of space to think about his life.

"I only take up a little bit of space," he said.

Soren went white and sobbed.

"But we are only little, you have to wait for us to be adults," he kept saying.

I took them out for pizzas, and quietly vowed to myself to get my marriage back on track.

So I flung myself back at Husband Three, unable to tolerate the painful reality of separation or the children's frightened sorrow. Before long, we had agreed to put our wedding rings back on. Two months later, the kids and I moved back to our house in the forest.

I tore myself apart trying to figure out how to make us love each other, trying to pin down the faulty gene, the broken fibre, the loose connection. But soon we fell back to our default setting – cold, separate, remote, our pent-up anger festering in sulky gloom, with me chattering nervously, meeting his taciturn silence. Every small rejection felt like a body blow. It was a twisted melodrama that ravaged my confidence and self-image.

Looking back, I realise Husband Three had actually checked out emotionally years before, and taking us back gave him more time to make proper plans for himself. He made it clear I was unwanted – an ageing woman who wasn't good at housework or cooking, and who wasn't even willing to financially sponsor his artistic ambitions and lifestyle. The boys sided with Team Mum and were fiercely protective, running to stand right next to me during his many verbal attacks on my personality. Husband Three believed I was indulging the children, so was extra strict to compensate, and resented having to always play the 'bad cop'.

His passive aggression was relentless. He'd push my buttons then step back and watch when I reacted. He sulked on planned outings. He'd disappear in theme parks and the boys and I were left to enjoy the entertainment not knowing where he had run off to. Every outing I planned to show him what fun being a family was ended up with me in tears and Husband Three stony-faced. His complaints were endless – it was too hot, there were too many people, our kids too needy, he didn't have enough food, there was too much walking, the kids were curtailing his fun, I was too bouncy, too fast, too impatient.

After we returned from our first separation, we all sat round the dining table, and I told the boys: "Mummy and Daddy won't ever divorce, I promise we will always be together – a real family."

As I looked up, I was struck and chilled by Husband Three's uncomfortable look of dis-ease. No matter what I tried, he stone-walled me, not involving me in any way in his life, either work or leisure.

I was so in love with my idea of a family. Ironically, it was my plan to have family portraits on the beach one perfect early summer evening that signalled the final end. Husband Three was fuming with rage at having to make time in his schedule for the photo shoot.

"Pretend you love me," I hissed. "Please, just put your arm around me."

The photographer, looking increasingly uncomfortable and nervous at the obvious tension radiating between us, concentrated on the boys and wrapped the shoot up quickly.

I refused to read the writing on the wall, that for Husband Three our marriage was dead and over. His method of escape was to be so unpleasant that he hoped to force me to crack and leave him.

Then, finally, there came the sign, the final straw, that it was the end. I had to go. Husband Three started to take his frustration and anger out on our children. On several occasions, the kids were smacked across a room. They were so afraid, they pee'd in their pants. Then one day, he boxed my youngest son's ears. I fled and hid away with the boys for a few days to let the situation defuse.

Within six months of getting back together, we were apart again.

I hired lawyers. Husband Three was ordered to remove his belongings, and our house was put back on the market. We sold up at an enormous financial loss, I let him take assets I thought I was entitled to in our property settlement in case he made good on his threat to go for shared custody, and we started divorce proceedings.

But I wasn't prepared for how sad I was to give up my dream of the traditional nuclear family, how torn my children would be, and how financially ravaged I would become. I was swamped in bitter confusion and overwhelmed with how old and useless I felt. I looked in the mirror and saw a wrinkled and frumpy failure.

It wreaked havoc on my kids.

My boys didn't care if Mum and Dad weren't happy together. They just want to be a family. My eldest son still cries about the split. Two years after we separated, he was still writing in his school diary about his weekends where Mum, Dad, himself and Soren spent blissful days frolicking about together. As a result, his teacher was surprised to hear we were in fact divorced by then.

Now their dad has a girlfriend, and they find it all very awkward and confronting, mainly the sexual vibe and kissing stuff that goes on. And it doesn't help that, despite all the warnings every expert has given, telling separated parents to pretend to get on for the sake of the kids, not to use kids as pawns or disrespect the other partner, we were initially not at all successful. Until recently, it was impossible for Husband Three and me to maintain a civil conversation, and I know the naked hostility has hurt our sweet babies.

"Dad said marrying you was a mistake," Yannik said on a car trip coming home this year. "He says you weren't kind to him."

Startled, I tried not to stoop so low as to defend, but merely trotted out my cliché that meeting their dad, falling in love and getting married meant that he and Soren got to be born – which made his dad and me very happy because "We both love you boys very, very much".

"Not true," he replied. "If you and Dad hadn't met, you would've had kids with some other man. I stole some other child's place. We weren't supposed to be born."

"If anything happened to you two boys," I said, "I would die. It would be like someone cutting away my heart."

Clearly this is something he had been thinking about for some time.

"Nah," he said. "Benjamin died and you survived quite fine."

I just stopped the car, got out and pulled him into my arms.

"Listen to my heart talking to yours – can you hear the love?"

My little one started yelling that he wanted to hear it too. So the three of us stood on the side of the road and hugged until the boys started complaining that I was squeezing them too tightly.

Having children made the end of this marriage more complicated than losing a husband to death. Death is final. You have to deal with it. But divorce is a choice. The illusion of marriage, with all its fairy-tale promises of united love and supportive security and unity, was very hard for me to give up on.

Separating nearly destroyed me. Unlike my fantasy, it was not about freedom and the option to do what you want when you want with no one putting you down or cramping your unique style. In reality, none of the preconceived ideas felt good any more. All my fanciful divorce treats now seemed too difficult, too expensive, too fatiguing, too much hassle. My life of freedom no longer seemed fun. It looked like a terrifying abyss of solitary bitterness. I became imprisoned by rage and poverty, immobilised by miserable indecision and thoroughly exhausted by the emotional effort divorce took with all the legal and personal tangles. Yes, even when I made the effort to get out there and attended a few music festivals with the boys, being surrounded by people having a good time, I was paralysed by self-pitying misery.

I did not imagine myself at the age of 50 as the separated, single and celibate mum of two young sons, with no viable man on the horizon, with the prospect of having to work for the rest of my life. Broken and insecure, I was frightened. It was heartbreaking and one of the toughest experiences I've survived.

Like everyone else, my separation followed the usual pattern. One minute I felt happy and relieved to be free, then I'd sink into fear and despair at what would happen to me and my kids. I bounced between manic highs and lows, sometimes many times in one day, drinking too much, laughing too long and loud, and crying a lot. Then the fury set in, from bitter hatred to anger, spreading out to many areas of my life and incorporating a wide range of people, innocent or not. And once again, I felt so alone and scared.

Chapter 21

The world shows a lot of compassion when there is a death. But for a crisis like divorce, I found myself on my own. The two years leading to the legal end of my marriage were mostly desolate, confusing and wretched. It wasn't just the loss of my dream of a family, but the brutal end of my children's innocent security.

The day our beautiful tree house in the forest sold in May 2012, I chucked my job in, bought a camper van and took off with the kids into the Australian Outback. I had to flee to find space, and lick my wounds. We'd been separated six months and divorce papers were being drawn up.

In true Monica style, our trip was spontaneous. After the sale of our forest home, my sons and I first took a trip inland to look at an interesting city simply because we'd never been there before. On the way there, we saw a road sign that said: Darwin 3 500km.

"Where's that, Mum?" Soren asked.

"It's at the top of Australia in the Northern Territory," I answered.

"Let's go there," the kids said.

So we went home, packed up our stuff and put it into storage and bought a little caravan. Two days later, we were back on the highway heading out of town. Two hours into the trip, I realised the caravan was really heavy and our car was struggling to tow it. Just then, I saw a second-hand car yard selling a camper van. I swapped the caravan for the camper van and the owner arranged a place for my car to be stored. We moved our small bundle of possessions from one home to the next, and two hours later, papers signed and licences sorted, we were off again.

We moved from the stress into an expansive panorama of grain silos, an endless sea of blonde grass swaying in the breeze, bottle trees, gum trees with white bark, psychedelic greens and purples, dead kangaroos, birds of prey, roadhouses and glorious red-orange sunsets.

The further I move from the Gold Coast, the more I smiled. The tension in my belly slowly unravelled; freedom and joy seeped back and my bounce returned. Hanging with packs of Grey Nomads restored my faith in happily married couples interacting harmoniously, loving companionships built on years of commitment.

"Been livin' in our van side by side for a year travellin', and we're doing pretty good," one 78-year-old husband told me. "We've raised four kids, stuck it out together through life's ups and downs, now we're livin' the dream."

We shared tips on free camping sites, worthwhile places to visit, where we'd been and where we were going.

When I forgot myself, I was happy. For so long I had felt trapped by the overwhelming Hinterland forest on one hand, social expectations and concrete buildings, traffic and endless routines on the other. I had felt like a hamster on a wheel, around and around and around. I've never been comfortable trapped by suburban lifestyle, domestic duties and routine. I like a base camp to centre me, but staying put suffocates me. I see life as an adventure and I don't want to miss out on a moment imprisoned by conventional expectations. So getting out and away was such a massive relief. My motto became: Mad before, Nomad today.

The kids wrote diaries, blogged, researched destinations online, and completed Maths workbooks as we travelled. We stopped at museums, hung out with bush folk writing poetry and singing round fires. We went on a dig for dinosaurs in Winton, and travelled through unspoilt lands, where imagination can run freely as you look out over the horizon, watching it blend into the sky in the foggy distance. We stopped at quirky roadside cafés, like the Pink Panther Roadhouse with its free zoo and outback artefacts. We'd drive, stop, look and listen. Trees became shorter, sparser, soil turned red, the haze increased, termite hills grew as tall as bushes, and life became languid.

Longreach on the Tropic of Capricorn is home to the School of Distance Education, the Australian Stockman's Hall of Fame and The Qantas Museum – all iconic outback experiences before heading off to view the massive cattle stations. Then onto Cloncurry and Mt Isa in the Gulf Country, famous for the single most productive mine in the world, and an oasis of civilisation among the silver-lead-zinc rocks. Down the highway we continued, to Camooweal, where multicoloured sandstone hills surround the centre of enormous cattle drives across the territory.

The boys climbed forward and backward in the van, sleeping or chatting. We'd play I-spy, count road kill, wave to everyone who passed, sing road songs, and read to each other. When the boys lay in the back to sleep or study, I'd drive and think, vaguely chatting in circles to myself about where I am going and why and when and how. I sought to patch back the essential bits of my heart I'd lost over the last two decades, trying to work through my disappointments. The more time I spent in my bubble of road-trip haze, the more I justified why keeping my kids out of school for a while was A GOOD THING. In an ever-changing, moving world where change is fast and relentless, I wanted my boys to be able to adapt mega-quickly. And they certainly showed how quickly they could familiarise themselves during a quick stopover at the Bitter Springs Thermal Pools at Mataranka deep into the Northern Territory. Travellers stop at the natural spring-fed pools to soak in the soothing warm waters in the dappled light of the forest. People can also float gently from the pools, and down the Roper River a couple of hundred metres to a bridge, climb out on a rickety ladder, then walk through the paperbark and palm woodland back to the pools again. Within the hour, my kids were running informative floating tours from pool to bridge, pointing out the hidden trees and logs, pointing out the flying red foxes and discussing surrounding flora and fauna they had read about en route.

A few weeks later, we reached the top of Australia – the balmy and funkilicious Darwin. As we drove into town, we stopped at the main stretch of beach to have a picnic before finding the local camp site, chomping down on our hamburgers, looking longingly out at the bright blue water sparkling in the 30-degree sunshine.

"Can we swim, Mum?" Soren asked. As we stood there thinking about it, Yannik pointed to a sea eagle scanning the water. Next thing, as it dived down to grab a fish, out of the corner of my eye, I saw a big movement, then SNAP. A crocodile had jumped up and snapped both the bird and the fish.

We looked at each other in complete shock. Locals also watching nearby agreed that it had been a crocodile. We took turns looking through binoculars to see the nostrils poking up in the water.

"I have changed my mind – I don't wanna swim any more," Soren said.

I tried to imagine it sweltering in the humid summer months, me with sweat dripping off my nose and flies and mosquitoes eating me alive … in a bid to put myself off the desire to stay there forever. But it was a winter paradise. The long and smooth bike paths take cyclists from town to the suburbs; public facilities are large, clean and varied. We revelled in Waterworld and wave pools, museums and galleries, outdoor café society, glorious Asian-style restaurants, the fabulous Mindil Markets, and truly perfect sunsets that turned the entire city a rich red.

We took trips down to Kakadu and Litchfield national parks, which look like parts of the Kruger Park and I half expected lion and elephant and giraffe to appear. We lay on the sandstone ledges under tropical waterfalls, skipped stones in the swimming holes and climbed magnetic termite mounds.

I had to *drag* myself away from the Territory, kids kicking and screaming, and promised to return soon. So back we went … retracing our steps to Mt Isa, leaving the land where you have to show your ID card when buying alcohol (in case you are on the Banned Drinking List!) and you have to show your ID card and hand over car keys at petrol stations (in case you drive away without paying!) where white women in fancy 4x4s flash electric smiles (false) when they pass Aboriginal folk while clutching handbags closely to their sides. So many things to distinguish white folk from Aboriginal from Asians (yip, all the vastly different Asian countries plunked under one cultural umbrella) – and definitely an US and THEM mentality going on. It was so South Africa in the '70s.

We passed roadside stops every 120 kilometres or so, road trains and road kill, signs welcoming us to the Never Never Land, while listening to horseracing on TAB radio, the only channel with reception. As I drove, my mind drifted, wondering why some people can make order from chaos while I am only able to turn order into chaos. I just held onto the faith that I had no idea where I was going but I would hopefully end up where I am meant to be.

Every kilometre I drove, the gloomier and sicker I felt to be moving out of the red and into the beige. As we crossed into Queensland (after solidly driving for over 1 000 kilometres) I seriously contemplated turning around and going back. But I am not a person for retracing my steps, so it was onwards, forwards, towards my destiny. After the brilliant display of day-glo greens and reds, yellows and oranges, the weather became cold with an icy wind, the scenery became bland and boring with savanna grassland endlessly stretching out with the midday sun bleaching the landscape of all rosy hues.

I taught in a high school in the mining town of Emerald for a few weeks and my boys went to the primary school.

"Where d'ya live?" the kids at school asked mine.

"In our van in the park," they replied.

"No seriously, where d'ya REALLY live?" their classmates persisted. "Where's ya house?"

"Nowhere," my kids replied. "We haven't got a house."

It rained the whole time. We were living in our van, and the kids were soaking and sick. When Yannik and Soren both got a stomach bug with vomiting and diarrhoea, I knew it was time to find us a home again.

But where to go? I drew up lists with pros and cons. I tossed coins. I felt lost. In the end, I gravitated back to the Gold Coast as my dear friend, Fiona from my Dead Baby Society, had just been diagnosed with breast cancer and I wanted to be near her and other friends. Plus, my sister Catherine still lived there.

Moreover, part of me was still connected to Husband Three on a fundamental level and sort-of hoped that I'd return and find out both our personalities had completely transformed, our history would be forgotten and a miracle would forge us back together. Legally, if we ever had a custody showdown, I feared the law might encourage me to move close enough for them to have a relationship with their dad. His occasional texts that found their way to me were filled with love.

"I have been thinking of you a lot," he said. "I would love to see and talk to you."

He assured me he was not dating, nor had he slept with anyone else. I believed him.

So I headed back to the Gold Coast and bought a little house in the suburb of Nerang, found a job again at my old school teaching English to foreigners and, once again, thanked myself for the foresight to get out of print journalism.

But settling back on the Gold Coast meant facing reality again – my lonely life without a husband, on the verge of being a divorcee. It was clear he was quickly detaching and emotionally leaving me forever.

Most of 2013 was spent wrapped in suffocating swathes of toxic hate – towards myself, towards life, towards everyone, but mainly towards Husband Three for not being the person I wanted him to be.

I really loathed myself for failing in marriage. I felt that so much of my life had been insufferable, and I was haunted by regret and painful memories and wasted opportunities. It wasn't the loss of my actual Husband Three, but the loss of a husband in general. I wanted to belong to someone, and to have a man of my own.

The end of Marriage Three ripped open wounds from the death of Ken to Steven and Benjamin – and the pain of all these tragedies came flooding back again. The wardrobe containing my emotional luggage, packed so tightly and carefully away over the years, was yanked open and all my stuff came tumbling out and crashing down. The power surge caused my lights to trip and my life was plunged into shadows. Living was bleak, a chore to be endured.

Getting to work required a double espresso every morning, then I'd have panic attacks driving to work, a teaching job I really love.

One morning I stood outside my school crying so much I was unable to move. I phoned a colleague.

"Help," I said. "I'm standing outside but I can't teach today. I can't move. I think I'm having a nervous breakdown."

"Nonsense," she replied briskly. "We're casuals … no work, no pay … Catch the lift up here right now or I will come and drag you up."

By the time my students walked into class, I had managed to plaster on a smile and appear upbeat and nah-nah perky again.

But in the dark, my body felt heavy with grey disillusionment, the stench of abhorrence seeping out of every pore, tears creeping out even at night and soaking my pillow of broken dreams, and I flopped around the house, unable to sleep, with shoulders hunched, slumped forward in defeat. I was pathetic.

In the two years of separation, Husband Three and I still communicated nearly every day, and I felt like we were in a holding pattern, that our separation was merely a respite from the train smash of our marriage. I couldn't accept that he didn't love me any more and I certainly wasn't actively planning a life without him. I had no idea of how we would possibly make it work – I was repulsed by every part of him – but I also was really attached to the idea of us being together and raising our sons. It also didn't help that the oldest man I had ever been with was Husband Three, by now 40 years old, and dating men in my age group was a hideous thought.

I did try a few but frolicking about with men in my age group was not a pretty sight. When a few shrivelled pink penises were put on brief display, I wondered if it were me, now so old and repulsive. In retrospect, it probably had more to do with the fact that one man had a serious drink-drug problem and was being investigated by the police, the other was a depressive with prostate cancer, and another was quite sweet but about to have heart surgery. I enjoyed a further few coffee dates that proved pleasant but with no potential, just oldish men whingeing about sore backs and knees. For my part, having two very young sons emotionally and financially dependent on my time and money meant I was not hugely attractive to the opposite sex either.

For the first two years, life as a single mum was so confronting and daunting, I flung myself back at Husband Three, crying that it was all a big mistake and begged him to take us back.

"I'll change," I promised. "I'll be good and kind and cook and give you all my money and work every minute of the day serving you … just come back to us."

I was a wreck. I felt ashamed, embarrassed, frightened. But the more he stonewalled me, the more I clung, I screamed, I begged, I felt severely abandoned and betrayed. I'd go over the same ground endlessly, trying to come at it from different angles, trying to break through his wall of disconnection. But only I was talking. Then I was shouting.

I felt my life had shattered into shards of glass. I was filled with recriminations. Could I have given him more attention, been a better wife, loved him more, laughed at him less? I was too old, too ugly, too fat. Why did Ken have to die? Why did Steven have to leave me? Now Husband Three too?

The begging and crying was a low and shameful patch but, as it happens to so many of us divorcees, I try to forgive my loss of dignity and move on. I think it was the look of boredom and pity mixed with irritation on his face that cut me to the quick.

We finally got officially divorced, 10 years after we married, on 4 October 2013, two months before my 50th birthday. I threw a divorce party with girlfriends and we all dressed up in our wedding dresses and held a fun quiz evening with lots of giggles and silly photographs. We even had an un-wedding cake with a figurine of a bride holding the bleeding head of her ex by the hair. But I felt like such a loser.

Husband Three then announced he had a serious girlfriend and he was introducing her to the kids. I nearly fainted with shock and, once again, plunged into the depths of neediness.

"Please give us another chance again ... Please, please don't do this to us," I howled, clinging to him in the road outside our home where he was trying to collect the kids.

Husband Three simply replied that he didn't want to go there, and that he couldn't see us together again.

"Never, ever?" I pleaded.

"Well, I've learnt never to say 'never' but I can't imagine it," he replied.

He then left for his weekend with the kids. Smiling bravely, I waited for them to drive out of sight before falling to pieces and sobbing. Once I got it together, I decided to drive down the coast to visit my sister, but was soon sobbing my eyes out again, emotional pain level probably around 8 out of 10.

"I'm too sad to cope with the pain," I thought. "How can I kill myself? How can I get a gun? Will I die today?"

I wasn't helped by the fact that the sentimental love duet "Perhaps Love" with John Denver and Plácido Domingo was playing in the background ... sob ... so I turned the radio to the news and soon was driving along again quite happily.

I went on to have a lovely day on the beach with my sister, giving no thought to suicide or ending life and feeling perfectly happy. Driving home later, I wondered why I was begging to go back to someone who clearly loathed me and who I disliked right back, a mismatched partner who had annoyed and hurt me most of my marriage.

I deeply loved, admired and respected Ken and Steven for so many reasons, and never much liked Father of Kids (FOK) most of the time, so why was it so hard to make the break? But he was the father of my children, my husband, the one man who was supposed to love and support me unconditionally. My grief was crushing. My horror of being discarded like an old, unwanted handbag was overwhelming.

But my emotions were up and down like a kangaroo on amphetamines. By the time Husband Three dropped the kids off that same weekend, I was out on the road, crying again, asking him what I should do with all my pain and fear, how to pick up and move on. Husband Three just stood there and looked at me.

"Say something – feel free to give me advice … What the fuck should I do? Help me!" I pleaded.

"I don't know what to say," he said. "I don't know what to do to help."

He left. I lay my head on the outside table and sobbed uncontrollably. In the background, I heard the kids playing computer games, oblivious to the drama going on with their mum.

So, as I often did, I headed off down the road to my neighbour, Kimbra. She called the other neighbour, Jonene, to help cheer me up. I was fed a few tranquilisers, we all drank a few glasses of wine, smoked a cigarette or two, and ordered pizzas for the kids. In fact, my boys were even allowed to have ice cream and chips that night, a very rare treat for emotional emergencies only.

I awoke at dawn feeling stupid, embarrassed, hungover and tight-chested. The boys had put themselves to sleep and I found them cuddled down in Yannik's bed the next morning, so I added mother-guilt to the bubbling cauldron of self-hatred and pity.

Thank goodness, like many powerful feelings, my attachment to the idea of our marriage completely dissolved over the year and our only bond now is through our children. We communicate through SMS with occasional phone conversations. I'm astonished at how quickly he's become a stranger.

The very worst part about divorce is losing my children four days a fortnight to a parent who has a completely different style and attitude to raising children. I agonised about my loss of control, was and still am dreadfully jealous of his hours with them, concerned about stuff they told me they were being exposed to, and utterly furious he was taking them away from me.

I now want to slap the people who suggest that my continued dislike of Husband Three is due to "not being over him".

I am still pissed at him for being such a disappointment, though now I can accept that the man couldn't help being who he is. I barely bothered to get to know him, and he was right that I didn't respect him because comparisons are so unkind.

"You wouldn't hate him if you no longer had any feelings for him," I've heard it said.

Yes, I do have feelings for him, but sadly, any bonding and tender memories have been drowned in mutual humiliation and fury during the divorce.

Experience tells me that this too will pass as the intensity of memory fades with the passing of time.

Chapter 22

My transformation from South African patriot to Aussie national has been surprisingly challenging, with the cultural gap much larger than anticipated, changing the fundamental building blocks of my psyche. While everything else has been going on in my life, I've also had to confront who I fundamentally am. I'm no longer a South African but now a South African-born Australian, a very different creature indeed.

Since arriving in Australia, I became a mother again, a wife again, then a divorcee – and all the while settling into a new country, and with so many massive changes, sometimes it was hard to keep track of who I was.

Part of me is still very much Saffa – and I'm remarkably proud when 'we' do well in anything. Even the news story of the fake deaf signer at Nelson Mandela's funeral – the crazy man with dangerous and violent episodes who made his way right next to 90 of the world's top world leaders – made me feel proudly South African.

"Ha ha ha … only in South Africa," I giggled to my friends. "Yeah!"

But this is starting to change and, as my South African life becomes more distant, my allegiances have changed. I'm now a big fan of Australian rugby codes like Australian Football League (AFL) and Australia's unique National Rugby League (NRL), as opposed to Rugby Union, which South Africans grow up on. I do believe Australia is the 'lucky country' and I am very privileged to be raising my children under this big, clean and beautiful blue sky where possibilities are endless.

While the climate and English language may be shared by the two countries, the culture shock of moving to Australia was surprisingly big. I still worry about raising my children in Australia because of my perceptions of the lackadaisical education system where I believe children have a comparatively weak determination and low tertiary schooling ambitions. Most South African-born Australians send their children to private schools to protect them from academic mediocrity.

Because it's traditionally a country of the working-class people with strong trade union traditions, tradesmen are cashed-up, and thus academic ambition isn't very important to many Australians. I fear my children will become too casual about life, complacent about their place in the world, without the urgency and sense of motivation South African children tend to have. I am concerned my boys will develop a sense of entitlement, that the government owes them, that they will think Centrelink Benefits and Medicare are their right, not a luxury.

While crime in Australia can't be compared to South Africa, this is not a perfectly calm paradise. Five young people were arrested right next door to me recently for allegedly running a crime syndicate and cooking crystal meth. The boys had guns tattooed on their faces and they all had clearly been sampling their wares. Plus, a smackhead, on his way to get his fix from the methadone clinic nearby, once put his hand in my ground floor apartment window and walked off with my laptop. But that said, I don't know one person who has been robbed while at home, nobody who has been carjacked, and I know nobody who even knows anyone who has been beaten or murdered.

Another negative is the level of racism in Australia. There is far too much talk about the Yellow Peril, fear of the wave of Asian immigrants. The Australian 'whites-only' policy has been revoked since 1973, but its spirit lives on in quite a large number of old-timers. These days, the present Australian government's aggressive "Turn Back the Boats" campaign to keep out humanitarian refugees coming in via rickety, old and overcrowded people-smuggling ships so popular with voters at the moment really worries me. As for the Aussies who sidle up to me and say, "You Saffas knew how to keep your darkies in their place – see what's happening in South Africa NOW," I want to slap them. I am also utterly shocked at how many white Australian-born Aussies blithely refer to black South Africans using the dreaded K word.

Yet each time I return to visit South Africa, I feel increasingly foreign. I am now frightened by the crime, more and more depressed by the deteriorating infrastructure and worry for the safety of my South African family and friends. I am too old and tired now to whip up the required adrenalin and stamina to live in South Africa. Australia has made me soft. More and more, I feel that I, with my white skin and English heritage, fit better here in Australia than in South Africa. South Africa no longer feels like a country I can identify with any more and I don't feel entirely welcome.

Australia, bar the one per cent of Aboriginal people, is a land of immigrants. More and more of us come from countries where lifestyles are more challenging, and share difficult personal stories of survival. My friends include Iranian Bahá'ís with stories of untold horror, Afghanistanis, Sri Lankans who fled from Tamil Tigers, Sudanese and Congolese ... the list is long and multi-cultural. Immigration is now so diverse and extensive that towns are awash with people from all around the world. In 2011, the Census reported by the Australian Bureau of Statistics revealed that over a quarter (26%) of Australia's population was born overseas and English is not their first language. A further one fifth (20%) had at least one overseas-born parent.

But I also am South African enough to need frequent contact with the increasing number of South Africans flocking here to ensure I feel balanced and centred. I need to touch base with like-minded people with a similar upbringing and shared history. It's then I know who I am – an English-speaking South African Australian. And I do feel an overwhelming sense that I finally fit.

What I love most about Australia is the sense of community I never felt in South Africa. Yes, those who worked in the South African media were like a family, bonded by shared experiences over the years. But the gentle sense of neighbourliness in my neighbourhood is hard to beat.

For those not familiar with suburban culture on the Gold Coast in Queensland, let me explain: the suburb I live in – Nerang – is not reputed to be a 'cool' area where classy and cultured people deign to live. When I arrived on the Gold Coast 10 years previously, the one thing I was told right off was that Nerang was *not* the place where sensible or decent people lived – it was where (cue the scary music) Nerangatans hung out; home central for dirty drongos, druggies and dole bludgers ... you know, the 'funny' (and not the more acceptable funny-ha-ha) people.

But when I got divorced, it was the only place I could afford to live.

My 'burb is a hotbed of odd people – many of whom hang out at our local mall, the supermarket centre of broken dreams. Like every community, we have our own Mr Stink, who wears the same clothes day in and day out, summer and winter and visits the centre every day from 8.30am to 10pm Monday to Saturday rain or sunshine. We also have an overweight 70-year-old woman who proudly steps out in her fluorescent bikini and sarong (yellow or pink depending on her mood) with tropical flowers in her long and flowing grey-blonde hair where she struts up and down the aisles with the confidence of a supermodel. Then there are the Criminal Brothers, skinheads always sans shirt or shoes, the determined woman marching knees up and arms swinging from bin to bin collecting tins for recycling; the bald but bearded woman, the drunken cyclist, me sometimes in my pyjamas ... oh, it's a veritable circus of who's who in the Crazy Kingdom.

But it's also a warm and nurturing community. Most of us mums – yes, we all know each other from the school run through our kids – are unemployed or part-time workers, naturally, since this isn't the neighbourhood for career superwomen breaking through glass ceilings – though I have broken quite a few glasses and ceilings … and windows too actually, but I digress! The point is, we know the check-out tellers by name, dance with the marvellous manager from the bottle store, and if anything or anyone stranger than usual turns up, it's duly noted. In fact, my elderly neighbour photographs anyone suspicious – in case they are ever needed for police identification. This is also the neighbour who takes my rubbish bins in and out of my yard when I am away or I forget. So yes, we *know* our neighbours and are always willing to pitch in and help one another.

And our facilities – all within walking distance – are pretty impressive. We live right next to a state forest so we have hikes and trails on our doorstep, we have some awesome parks with hot water and free barbecues that are always clean, and the best and cheapest movie house in the country. Nerang has a massive swimming pool complex and a plethora of fancy gyms, none of which is overcrowded. We are within a 20-minute drive to mountains and beaches, and house prices give the best bang for buck, which means I can afford a house where the mortgage is lower than rent. There is a massive river running through the centre of town where kids fish, we have an excellent skateboard park with awesome jumps, a BMX track and an Olympic-quality cycling velodrome. I personally *love* our library with free wi-fi and conference facilities, and know all the staff there by name.

But it's the mums on my block who saved my sanity in 2013. Even though I only teach mornings, I was struggling to juggle the morning school run and getting to my job on time, so the mums rallied around and one phoned another and now someone down the road lifts my kids, the same woman who babysits the neighbour's dog each day so Fido isn't home alone barking.

Our special Mothers' Club meets in our street every Friday. Five or so mums walk over to somebody's house – we rotate – with our kids, hampers of food, bottles of wine, beers and ciggies. The kids play and we party. Ex-husbands come round to pick up the kids on alternate weekends, and stay awhile, mine excluded. And when one of us freaks out – hard day, feral kids, small disaster – we all step into the fray and help. When I had a knee operation after falling off a cliff while camping, the mums fetched my kids and fed them.

So Nerang – named on our rates notices as Sherwood Forest Estate – is certainly not boring. Its spirit is reminiscent of my beautiful memories of Nelspruit in Mpumalanga. This too is a rainbow of multicoloured madness. It's a human kaleidoscope of multifaceted reality right on our doorstep, with a warm and friendly ambiance to wrap around my daily existence.

So, while I am essentially South African-made, I've also become proudly Aussie. And it can feel strangely confusing.

Chapter 23

"I don't know how you survived what you have ... you are so strong ... you are an inspiration."

Since the death of Benjamin, following the death of Ken and then Steven, people occasionally remark on their surprise that I survived the dark days and wonder how I did it. The answer is: I don't really know. But I do know that if someone like me can make it, anyone probably can. I don't think it had anything to do with strength of character or courage. It is more the basic innate instinct to pull through and move on. It's a case of letting go and not looking back. But I also believe everyone deals with grief differently, and that no advice fits all. I can just write about what works for someone like me.

When Ken died, I was still a relatively young woman with so much to look forward to. I initially fell apart and stepped off the edge a few times, but fortunately just low ledges as opposed to an abyss. Still, I was not okay. And when Steven died, I had my darling Benjamin to live for. When Ben died, I had no idea how I was to live with the pain. However, my innate desire to find meaning and love in my life forced my mind to do extraordinary things – meeting and marrying a man with whom I had two children – before anyone could blink twice.

Mental health is not, and never has been, my closest friend.

I have spent a lifetime fending off and surviving endless attacks of the crazies – to the point I often bore or exhaust myself with the rapid up-down seesaw pattern of my life. So what keeps me bouncing back?

Firstly, the human body is amazing. Sometimes it's easier dealing with the big losses – death or divorce – because we are so stunned and our bodies react to protect us. When all tragedies struck, the chemicals in my body kicked in big time. With my incredible shock, the flight-or-fight chemicals flooded in, and adrenalin, cortisol and dopamine were pumped through my blood. The blood filled up with body-made opiates like oxytocin. Instantly, my ears started to ring, my head was swamped by a fuzzy cotton-wool fog and I was unable to hold onto any thought for more than a few seconds. As the first shock wave of pain hit, my body went into overdrive and sensibly closed down the brain and the central nervous system. The upshot is that I can't remember too much of the days following the deaths, just vague montages of moments flashing back gradually over the years.

Unfortunately, this chemical overload also threw my balance so I crashed cars, nearly sliced off a finger in the blender and generally blundered my way around for months on end. Research shows when people are very shocked, their ability to concentrate decreases and the immune system becomes vulnerable. Any non-essential bodily functions close down – so it became hard for me to gauge temperature, my hunger disappeared and my brain actually shrivelled up, making me very indecisive. I battled to recognise people, I couldn't remember even basic stuff, and I became stupid. When the protective chemicals waned and reality seeped through, the intensity of the pain soon forced my brain to shut right back off again.

Perhaps I have a super-strong rebound gene that assists in developing resilience – and this gives me a better ability to adapt and rebuild my life after tragedy. Certainly, getting emotional and geographical distance helped. Distraction was essential. Within a year of both husbands dying, I was remarried and living in another country. I also can't imagine surviving the death of Benjamin if I had stayed in a place where everyone and everything reminded me of my loss. For me, the more time and distance from the disaster, the easier it was to recover. It is true that emotional overload dissipates over time – and I filled my life with as much action, noise and general chaos as possible to distract me from my feelings until time had passed. I didn't allow time for sad reflection so I wouldn't sit around quietly listening to music or looking through photo albums. I have only now begun to open my bags of memories to write this book – and I've been in Australia for 11 years – and I find a lot has been lost deep in the labyrinths of my mind.

Family has been my major trump card. Every time there's been a problem in my life, my close-knit family has surrounded me with love and support. Dad and Gail have packed up more of my homes than I have after I fled from death. They were always there, calmly and lovingly sorting my life out, time after time. My mum in Scotland was also at the end of the phone any time, on the internet and writing letters, letting me know I was never alone. My pain was her pain. My siblings also stopped their lives to be there for me when mine went awry – and their many kindnesses kept me going. I was also very lucky to have fantastic in-laws, and am particularly close to my sisters-in-law both Oosterbroek and Hilton-Barber, which is a rare and precious gift.

Gratitude has also been a motif running through all my heartbreaks – taking comfort from stories of people who had worse experiences than mine – and counting my blessings. At all stages, I had overwhelming support from friends and family, money to give me options, the means to take some time off work. Many others recovering from tragedies don't have that luxury. When I feel like a victim, I look at people who have had it so much worse than I have – and it makes me feel thankful not to be them.

Humour helped me cope, recover and heal. It gave me a respite from emotional chaos and helped to release some of my anger and fear. Laughing gave me hope my life would be fun again; it reminded me of the joy in life, and was a way to continue celebrating my life. Many people did not understand my black humour, and some were offended by it. But I uphold the views of George Bernard

Shaw, who said: "Life does not cease to be funny when someone dies any more than it ceases to be serious when someone laughs."

I also found exercise to be a life saver. When the going got tough, I went running because it's really hard to cry and run fast at the same time. But I always ran with pounding electronic dance music – nothing quiet and gentle that would cause tears – and never jogged with just my thoughts, which I feared would quickly lead me into dangerous mental neighbourhoods from where I might not have safely returned.

Sometimes, if I was hysterically blubbering away, especially in the days when I realised my marriage to Husband Three was not going to work, I would look at myself in the mirror. Just the sight of my sad, woebegone face was enough to distract me and, within seconds, I was inspecting a suspiciously grey hair, a new wrinkle or blemish. I'm shallow that way.

After Ken and Steven died, I started smoking a few cigarettes in the evening with a few wine spritzers. I like to mix my wine with litres and litres of diet lemonade, which I know is very pleb, but I've never been an enthusiastic drinker. When I arrived in Australia with my "Breed Again Right Now Today" programme, I was soon the healthiest fittest 40-year-old in town! To anyone wanting advice, all I can say is: Take care of yourself. Eat healthily. Avoid excessive alcohol or prescription drugs, though occasionally they are a very useful circuit breaker when the grief becomes too exhausting to cope with.

Like many people, I sought out material to read about other people's similar misfortunes and I found it immensely reassuring to see my experiences were not unique. I learnt that radical emotional ups and downs every day for months were normal, that you can't speed up or avoid the healing process, and that if you try to avoid the pain, it will be waiting for you down the track.

I handled my pain in micro pieces, taking it out over the years bit by bit until I learnt to live alongside it. I would take my pain out from time to time and confront it, then when it got too much, my brain would snap back into numb mode and I would leave it for another time. But others I know have actively confronted their pain head on, and really experienced it in all its vicious fullness, staring it down and riding it to the bitter end. They seemed to heal faster than I did. I have a close Australian friend whose marital breakdown was similar to mine. Our husbands were best friends and we had our sons at the same time. Then, when Husband Three and I split up, her husband ran off with another woman. When the pain hit, she said, "Bring it on," and decided to embrace the emotional fallout in all its intensity. She confronted the fullness of her pain, she never shied away from it in any way, and it nearly ripped her to shreds. It certainly looked neither easy nor pretty, but two years later, she was okay again.

It's hard to know why I have had so many disasters in my life. How much was I personally responsible for the mayhem? I have spent so much of the last few years in Australia trying to work out how much was me, how much was fate and destiny, and how much was just plain bad luck. I've tried to make sense of my life. There are so many religious and philosophical opinions out there. Part of me realises it's partly a bad deck of cards with perhaps a dash of pre-destiny – but the fate was certainly possible. Another part realises that the choices my personality have led me to make have also contributed. I am not a victim but have been instrumental in the path my life has taken. I have now faced up to the responsibility of my part in my extreme life.

I chose Ken knowing he was a photographer – but I didn't realise quite how dangerous it would all turn out to be. From the time we met, I knew our lives would always be volatile and filled with action – and I actively chose that over my lovely, calm boyfriend who had done a good job in my early twenties protecting me from my crazy self.

Falling in love with Steven, a recovering drug addict, so hot on the heels of Ken's death, was certainly not sensible ... But – pause here for laughter – I really couldn't help it. That certainly led to eight roller-coaster years that left me giddy, disorientated and deeply unable to be the calm, relaxed earth mother I should have been. Perhaps if I had been less panicked about Benjamin's operation – yes, my fear of death was massive by that stage –

I might have kept a cool head and taken better care of him. Like all mothers of children who have died, I feel immense guilt for not protecting him better and wish I had done things differently. In retrospect, no matter how much I loved Steven, losing Benjamin was nearly too much to bear and had I known how it would have turned out, I would have run. The joy was not worth the pain.

And then marrying Husband Three less than a year after Steven's death (and a mere few months after Benjamin's death) could also have been deemed an irresponsible move. But in retrospect, breeding was of the essence since I was already past 40 years old. Husband Three did help me out with two beautiful boys (and an Australian visa). However, the viciousness of the divorce, the immense heartbreak and deep sadness that followed were a very high price to pay.

I wish I could be like the Buddhist monks and learn to detach from earthly things to live moment to moment in a non-possessive manner. But I'm the complete opposite. I also constantly tell myself that life is short and at my age every moment counts, so it's no good wasting valuable time on bitterness, regret and anger. But it's sometimes hard to rise above these destructive emotions.

Sometimes I try to look at the positives of death. If Ken hadn't died, I wouldn't have met and loved Steven. If Ben hadn't died, I wouldn't have come to Australia and had Yannik and Soren. But then, what if Steven had lived and we had raised Benjamin together and gone on to have a handful or two of other children? See, it's this never-ending circle that drives me to depression.

While my life has soared and tumbled along, I have tried to make sense of the reason for living, the place of God or a Higher Being in all of this.

Born into a Christian home, I wanted to follow suit but, despite my best efforts, I have never been able to get my head around the idea of Jesus being the son of God. I have, from time to time, hung out with conservative Islamic women and have appreciated how their lives can be really peaceful and liberating, rather than stifling. I appreciate the beauty of their customs where they are Queen of the Home and Ruler of the Household – a mother, a daughter, a wife – surrounded by family and friends, cocooned.

But I now think there is no one path in life, no one way to happiness, and that not all paths are simply good and bad. I raise my children in the Bahá'í faith, following the teachings of Bahá'u'lláh and his son `Abdu'l-Bahá', focusing on virtues and morality rather than ideology and dogma. But I like to sift through many theories and religions to find truths that resonate with my heart and soul, an epic voyage – a journey to enlightenment – seeking something I feel comfortable with. Like many Bahá'í, I am more interested in the basic rhythms of nature, of karma and old-fashioned morality – respect, honesty and decency – than doctrine. I also understand the concept of retribution, which is described in so many different ways in many different cultures: You reap what you sow. What goes around comes around. The Law of Cause and Effect. What you put out comes back to you.

This past Christmas I was going through a common 'poverty' patch and only had $100 to shop for groceries for the festive season. However, I stopped to put $20 in a basket for a disabled man busking at our local supermarket. My kids couldn't believe it.

"Mum, we can't afford it," they said.

So I reiterated the concept of karma to them. When we got home, I went to the post box and found an unexpected $500 cheque from the Education Department for whom I had occasionally done casual work. It appears I qualified for a holiday pay cheque. My kids were very impressed at how fast karma works!

"It's a miracle," the little one said.

I can't pretend to begin to explain the meaning of life – and survival – because my understanding of myself and reason for my existence is a constantly shifting paradigm I continue to explore and re-evaluate.

All I know is that nothing – not even your own opinions – stay the same for long.

And as for survival, as Charles Darwin said, it's not the strongest or most intelligent who survive, but those who can best manage change.

Chapter 24

Slowly, slowly I crawled out of the pit of my Christmas-day collapse. When my sons returned on Boxing Day, I made them laugh at "Mummy being dramatic again" and told them I was feeling much better. I forced myself to smile and giggle and play games. And soon the pretence became reality.

Gradually the dizzy cycles of circles within circles in my mind stopped turning so quickly and life began to focus. I began to see through the soupy fog and distinguish shapes and horizons.

I took myself off to see a therapist to discuss that flash of death-wish madness. A few pieces of advice snapped me out of my deep funk.

"A thought is only a thought – these come and go – it's actions that define who you really are," she said.

Whew! That meant when terrible dark notions seeped into my consciousness, I could merely observe them dispassionately and these brainwaves soon floated out my ear and vaporised.

"When you feel really bad, rate the level of pain and see how long it lasts," she advised.

And it turned out that on a bad day, in fact, I only felt moderately hopeless and down for perhaps half an hour. That certainly put my life in perspective.

And when I felt myself spiralling down, I took control and

steered my brain left and drove it sideways out the tunnel and up again.

Fortunately, I soon bored myself with my sad flopping about and whingeing. I got to the stage where I thought: Fuck It. Time to put on my Big Girl Panties. Time was racing by and I didn't want to waste another second. Just yesterday my kids were small and the marvel of motherhood was all I needed to sustain me. Now they are getting bigger and more independent. I didn't want to wake up ten years down the track and wonder why the hell I didn't get a grip earlier and make my life worthwhile again. I wanted to attack life with a big bang, not with the pathetic whimpering of a helpless victim.

I am learning to accept that the general disharmony born from clashing personalities means Husband Three and I will never like or understand each other. I still deeply resent having to share the children but have to accept that my boys have a right to belong to both parents. My boys love their dad unconditionally, and their father loves them right back, but in a different way to me. I see this when I watch my children run to throw their arms around him when they go for their weekends with their dad, and see how he kneels down to hug and kiss them goodbye when they leave. My rational brain is happy for my boys because they want and need their father. I can now see that if we hadn't divorced, Husband Three may have lurked on the periphery, leaving parenting to me. Actively hating Husband Three only distresses my boys and forces them to take sides. These days, I try to accept I can't and shouldn't tamper with that precious father-son relationship. I've had to let go.

I woke up in the middle of this year and my heart filled with the gentle rays of gladness. The winter of my heart was over and spring quietly moved in. I knew I was going to be okay. And so the seasons of my life moved on, again.

Like so many of us heading well down the path into the Valley of Old Age, I am struck down by the fear of death. I no longer feel like a beautiful woman whose life is stretching out before her with endless possibilities. I feel old and tired and often frightened.

189

I worry about my parents, who are now heading towards the big 80, and I realise time spent together now is deeply precious. And I am so shallow and vain, it kinda bugs me that my tits have fallen down somewhat, my bum flops down on the back of my thighs, and when I smile my eyes disappear into a sea of wrinkles. I also dread impending joint deterioration, back pain and menopause. Whoop-de-whoop. But I'm too lazy to do anything constructive – like slap on a bit of make-up, iron clothes, occasionally blow dry my hair or get off my fat arse and run – so clearly I am not that distressed!

My Mothers' Club organised a bit of a birthday bash for me – a bring-your-own-food-and-drink affair attended by an eclectic mix of a few friends invited at the last minute. I wore a tiara, we danced in my garden and ate lots of cake until the early hours of the morning. And I treasure the fun I have hanging out with my different groups of girlfriends – in cafés and malls, at the beach, hiking or simply hanging around our homes. Nothing fancy, just food and laughter and companionship.

In the first half of my 50th year, I've already had a lot of fun. I joined a touch rugby team and we won the league competition. I was awarded both Most Improved and Most Confused player. I went Barramundi fishing in the Bay of Carpentaria. I learnt to swim butterfly, swam naked in a warm lake in the pouring rain and hiked five hours to the top of a volcano. My sons and I went to a music festival on the beach and danced all day in the sunshine. I tried naked gardening in the moonlight listening to Bach's double violin concerto in D minor, I've booked flights to South Africa for my sons and me, locked in a cycling trip to Cambodia this Christmas, and bought seeds to grow herbs. Also, the process of writing this book has given me perspective and closure.

Wouldn't it be great if I could report that the events of my life have made me appreciate living more; that I have become a more evolved person and therefore a kinder, more patient version of my old self? Sadly, while there are slight modifications, I return to my base personality of slightly hysterical, over-the-top self-absorption, with sanity still as tenuous as ever. I have learnt, however, that everything we love and trust and treasure can be whipped away in a heartbeat, that life is really fragile, and that nothing stays the same. It's a case of adapt or die.

If this was a sentimental Hollywood-esque story, it would end where I run slow motion on a beach at sunset into the arms of a rich widower with all his own hair and teeth and a penis that worked. To be extra perfect, the man would be a tall, dark somebody wanting to raise my children and put them through private schools. Oh, and while I'm paddling in the wishing pond, if he had daughters who were about to give him grandchildren, I would get to be a step-granny too, which would really be the cream on top of the cake.

But for today, I am really perfectly happy simply raising my sons, teaching and writing, embraced by my family and the beautiful network of girlfriends I have built up across the world. I can't imagine seeking a romantic relationship again because I am content with me and my life. I don't really want or need a husband again. I think my heart is full enough. Eros can be too dangerous for me and requires more emotional vigour than I presently feel like conjuring up. It no longer seems at all important. But I know never to say never.

My life hasn't turned out the way I once hoped. Some parts were definitely better than others. It's been happier and more glorious than I possibly imagined; I've been overwhelmed by love and excitement and amazing times. Yes, there has been tragedy. But my life has so far been an incredible adventure – one I feel is only going to get better and better.

Recently when Soren's teacher asked my son what we did over one weekend, he replied: "Mum flew us to the moon on the back of a dragon."

Yannik tells people that life at home with his mum is like a circus.

"She is a little bit wild and weird … but in a good way," he says.

Both boys are academically bright and very sporty, exceptionally good storytellers with rampant imaginations, with lives full of mischief and laughter, and both adore an adventure.

This makes me feel extraordinarily pleased – I believe I am doing something right there – because they will be my legacy.

Am I happy? The answer is that a lot of the time I am warmly content, a great deal of the time I am thrilled with life's joy, and these days, it's only just very occasionally I feel sorry for myself. But, whatever my lot in life, I am proud to have always bounced back like a ball. To my utter astonishment and to the surprise of many, I am still so full of life and passion, loving the prospect of making my fifties positively Fabulous.

Through the struggle to make sense of my life, I've learnt that survival is both a curse and a miracle, that it's hard to die of a broken heart, and that our human spirit is hard to crush.

Life is not all grief, all joy, or all of any one thing. It is a mixture of stuff … and grief has shown me that even in suffering, there is so much love, support and merriment.

The trick is to surrender to the inevitability of change, to trust and accept that the dark days will pass, and open your arms to the infinite potential of love, life, loss and everything in between.

Life is what it is.

And as my children always tell me: "White Rabbit, No Returns."